BREAKING
THE
SPELL OF THE PAST
ENTERING
THE
JOYOUS NOW

Eve Delunas, Ph.D.

LIGHTWORK VISIONS
ENTERPRISES

BREAKING THE SPELL OF THE PAST:
ENTERING THE JOYOUS NOW
BY EVE DELUNAS

The ideas, suggestions, and techniques presented in this book are not intended to replace the recommendations of a licensed mental health professional or medical specialist.

© 2003 Eve Delunas, Ph.D.

Published by Lightwork Visions Enterprises
P.O. Box 221520, Carmel, CA 93922
www.lightworkvisions.com

Art Direction and Design by Parisa Ashrafi
Cover Illustration by Natasha Dierwechter

All rights reserved. This book may not be reproduced in whole or in part, without written permission from the author, except by a reviewer who may quote brief passages in a review; nor may any part of this book be reproduced, stored in a retrieval system, or transmitted in any form or by any means electronic or mechanical, including photocopying, recording, or other, without written permission from the author. Address all inquiries to Lightwork Visions Enterprises, P.O. Box 221520, Carmel, CA 93922.

ISBN 0-9742284-1-9

First Edition, 2003
Printed in the United States of America

9 8 7 6 5 4 3 2 1

To Roger, My Beloved

TABLE OF CONTENTS

EXERCISES

I have altered the names, locales, and other identifying
characteristics of individuals in order to protect
their privacy while preserving coherence.
Some examples used are composites of two or more cases.

ACKNOWLEDGMENTS

I am blessed with wonderful family, friends, and associates who granted me the gift of their time and expertise in the creation of this book. In particular, I wish to thank my husband, Roger Stilgenbauer, who has been my sounding board, my astute advisor, and my loving guide throughout this process. I am grateful to my Lightwork Visions cofounder, Joyia Felice, for being an ever-present source of inspiration and support, and for suggesting the title of this book. Thank you also to Ute Bender, Mary Welschmeyer, Andrea Mosca, and Barbara Nelson. I send each of you my love and appreciation for your wise and thoughtful input. This book is greatly improved as a result of your many helpful suggestions.

A big thank you also goes to Parisa Ashrafi for her beautiful book design, Natasha Dierwechter for her lovely cover illustration, and Chris Benzel for his lifesaving production expertise. The three of you do amazing work!

Barbara Liberty, a woman of many talents, has been an important part of Lightwork Visions since its inception. In addition to her computer expertise and her organizational skills extraordinaire, I thank her for taking the picture inside the back cover. Barbara, you are a gem!

I also extend my gratitude to Robin Anderson, my editor, who has contributed greatly to this work with her artful fine-tuning of the book. Thank you for guiding this book through its final stages with such competence, grace, and care.

And lastly, I wish to express my heartfelt appreciation to all of the special people with whom I have had the opportunity to work in my psychotherapy practice. You have been my best teachers. This book would not have been written if it weren't for you!

PREFACE

In my twenty-five year career in psychology, I have often found myself confronted with psychotherapy clients who are stuck repeating undesirable patterns of behavior despite their best intentions to change them. These courageous people are hurting deeply and seeking a way to find greater joy and fulfillment in their lives; many have great insight regarding the origins of their problems, yet they have not succeeded in creating the changes they desire.

Early in my career, I tried my best to help these people by applying the principles and techniques I had acquired in my years of study toward my doctorate in psychology and my license as a Marriage and Family Therapist. Over time, I identified some highly effective psychotherapeutic methods for helping people heal wounds from the past. I found with these approaches most people felt better and took steps in a positive direction; many clients even found they were able to stop engaging in certain long-standing, self-sabotaging patterns of behavior.

Yet, I began to recognize that these methods did not go far enough. New issues and concerns would often appear to replace those that had been resolved. Many clients were unable to sustain the experience of joy, peace, and fulfillment they were seeking for prolonged periods of time. It seemed we could continue forever to work on one problem after another, without ever reaching the ultimate goal of a happy life.

Because of this, I began to examine the ways in which psychology might be contributing to the problem-centered worldview of many of my clients. I concluded that psychology focuses predominantly on the realm of the mind and emotions, and that it is precisely our thoughts and the emotions they trigger that keep us struggling and lost in the darkness of our psyches. The more we analyze our problems, the more we identify with them. We become the labels psychology applies to us, from "codependent" to "bipolar disordered." We live in the past, seeking to understand the "why's" and "wherefore's" of our behavior, all the while providing our minds with the optimal breeding ground for cultivating negative emotions. We remain unconscious of our true nature and driven by the mind's desire to maintain dominance. Since our minds seek problems to justify their importance and ways in which to exert control over us, the very methods we use to find our way out of this shadowland (a term I use to represent the land of shadows from our past), keep us captive there in a nightmare of our own making.

This is not to say that the mind does not have its place as a valuable tool for dealing with many of life's activities. Rather, I assert that our out-of-control minds have created much psychological distress. Therefore, looking for our minds to solve the very problems our minds have helped to create is illogical. Our minds, like guards, keep us imprisoned in the dark recesses of our psyches. How can we expect these sentinels within to guide us to the light, when they require the darkness for their own survival? They feed on our doubts and fears, and gain life from our confusion and insecurities. Surely we cannot look to the mind to lead us safely into the light of clarity and contentment: It is against the mind's best interest to do so.

You might think of our unhappy lives as a haunting movie that keeps us spellbound, and psychology's goal as helping us change the movie so it is more to our liking by analyzing the script and replaying and dissecting the scenes we dislike. But this only intensifies our involvement with the story line and identification with the role we are playing in the film. Real change does not happen until we shift paradigms, step outside the dark movie theater into the light of day, and rouse ourselves from our trance-like state. In doing so, we awaken to our true nature—a vast, multi-dimensional being with unlimited, creative potential.

In my years of working with clients, I have discovered it is only our Enlightened Spirit that can truly awaken us from our unhappy dream and lead us home again to the temple of light and love that exists within each of us. Your dazzling, radiant Spirit awaits your call for guidance and support. It longs to reveal its secrets to you— the nature of your true essence, the goodness of your being, the stream of wonder in which you may choose to reside. It offers unconditional love and the wisdom of the ages. It is a beacon in the darkness, pointing the way to true healing and freedom from suffering.

This book parallels my journey of discovery as a psychotherapist as I crossed the bridge between psychology and spirituality. Part One: Spellbound in Shadowland, explains how our past can hold us captive. Using the "ghosts" analogy, I outline how and why we become haunted during the traumatic moments of our lives. You will have the opportunity to identify those areas in which you are spellbound, engaged in unconscious patterns of behavior that are self-sabotaging, and to understand the dynamics which are keeping these patterns active. Part Two: The Awakening, shows you how to align with your Enlightened Spirit in order to awaken from your trauma-induced spell into a state of pure aliveness and joy. Learn how to transcend the problem-orientation of the mind to access the radiance of your essential nature and live to its fullest expression.

My wish for you, dear reader, is that you will use this work as a guidebook for exploration and discovery as you become acquainted with the limitless beauty and unparalleled peace of your internal landscape. Once you become a more frequent visitor, or even a permanent resident, of this other dimension of self, you will find that everything in your life begins to be transformed. Your outer world becomes a more perfect reflection of the inner glow you embody—the magnificent light of your Spirit.

With love and blessings,

Eve Delunas
Carmel, California
March 28, 2003

INTRODUCTION

Melinda is an attractive professional woman in her early fifties who came to me for therapy after she and her third husband had decided to divorce. As she spoke of her failed marriages with much anger, frustration, hurt, and sadness, I noticed that she used the words "he turned his back on me" in describing what went wrong in each relationship. I asked Melinda to close her eyes, relax, and tell me about the first time someone she loved turned his or her back on her. Within moments, Melinda spoke of being abandoned as a three-year-old on her father's doorstep as her mother turned and walked away, not to re-enter her life for several years. Further exploration revealed that Melinda's father and a number of other adults whom she loved and trusted had also repeatedly turned their backs on her during her childhood.

As an adult, Melinda has re-created the theme of her childhood in each of her marriages. It is not that Melinda intentionally set out to have her husbands disappoint, reject, and turn their backs on her both emotionally and physically. Indeed, Melinda wants desperately to have a successful, loving, mutually-supportive relationship with a man. However, until Melinda awakens from the spell of her traumatic past, she is likely to perpetuate the same distressful theme that was central to her early years.

Like Melinda, many of us are imprisoned by our history, unconsciously repeating undesirable patterns of behavior that create suffering. As we enact the same unsatisfactory life drama over and over again, the characters and situations may change, but the role we play rarely varies. With each disappointment, our feelings of hopelessness and helplessness are intensified. We long to stop revisiting the same depressing themes and reliving the familiar

1

unhappy endings, but we feel lost and uncertain about how to revive ourselves from our waking nightmare.

While we are under the spell of our past, we are like automatons, going through the motions of life without really feeling and being vibrantly alive. We view our lives through lenses that focus exclusively on our problems. Often we imagine a catastrophic future, anticipating the worst possible scenarios. We may suffer from anxiety, panic attacks, depression, violent outbursts, avoidance of intimacy, or addictions to substances, sex, work, or spending. We remain in unsatisfactory jobs and disappointing relationships, complaining about how miserable we are, while blaming others for our unhappiness. We may experience multiple physical problems, each more debilitating than the last. Who can blame us for trying to numb ourselves to the pain of our mundane lives by watching television, drinking alcohol, or taking prescription drugs?

Many of us attempt to escape our distress by searching the past for a key that unlocks the door to a more joyful life. We may spend endless hours recounting each detail of our history to see if it provides a clue as to why we have problems, hoping that such insight will enable us to change our lives for the better.

Others of us look ahead, and decide that when we have a different job, the right partner, the perfect body, or the latest model sports car—then we can have and enjoy the life we desire. We cling to the belief that our happiness is just around the next bend.

Neither of these approaches can foster the real change we need. In its own way, each perpetuates our suffering, rather than eliminating it. The exit door from our living nightmare cannot be found in either the past or the future, for it exists only in the present. It is only in the now that we can awaken from our spellbound state to our inner beauty, power, and creative potential. As long as

2

we stay focused on what has already happened or what might happen, we will miss the way out of the darkness and into the light. Like train platform number nine and three-quarters in the Harry Potter books, it is easy to miss the passageway from discomfort to joy if we are not looking in the right place, and are not cognizant of what we want to find.

This book is meant to be a map you can use to explore your internal landscape and locate the enlightened pathway that leads to a new way of being. It will help you awaken from your negative entrancement and experience vibrant awareness and joyous living. It will guide you in ending long-standing patterns of self-destruction and self-sabotage, and assist you in creating the life you truly desire. Use this book to step out of your disappointing dream and into your magnificent Now. Use it to dispel the ghosts from the past, hiding in the shadows of your psyche, who maintain the spell that keeps you perpetually asleep to your own essential nature.

The Ghosts from Our Past Imprison Us

It is these shadowy figures from our past that rob us of joy and paralyze us with guilt, shame, doubt and fear. They imprison us with feelings of self-hatred and worthlessness. They extinguish our hopes and dreams. They brand us as unworthy of happiness. Unconsciously, we continue to create situations in our adult lives that re-activate our original feelings of rejection, failure, loss, anger, victimization, powerlessness, humiliation, unworthiness, terror, and despair; and even when we recognize that our success and happiness are being sabotaged, we feel powerless to stop the patterns.

What are the remnants of the past that our inner phantoms use to maintain their negative hold on us in the present? They are traumatic memories, highly charged with painful emotions, that we have tried to bury. They are the feelings we have disowned or repressed, such as anger, fear, shame, hurt, guilt, or grief, because we decided, at some point, they were dangerous or unacceptable. They are the introjected voices of the people who criticized or humiliated us when we were children or adolescents: parents, siblings, other relatives, teachers, or peers. They are the negative habits of thought about ourselves that we adopted during our early years: thoughts that we are bad, unlovable, incapable, or unworthy. These thoughts became the destructive voices within, forever calling attention to what is wrong with us and our lives, cautioning us to always expect the worst, and admonishing us to look for a dark cloud on even the sunniest day.

Your Spirit Illuminates the Way

Your magnificent Spirit illuminates the path of freedom from the past that holds you captive. By opening the door to your radiant essence, and allowing its splendor to flood your body, mind, and emotions, all illusions cast by your inner phantoms are dispelled in the light of clarity and higher wisdom. The ghosts that haunt you cannot survive in the presence of your Spirit.

Aligning with your radiant essence can enable you to fill your heart with love and forgiveness of self and others. Inner tormentors dissolve in the presence of true self-acceptance. In addition, the divine peace that permeates your being inoculates you against any efforts to infect your consciousness with doubts and fears.

As you become one with your Spirit, you will naturally focus on positive, uplifting, appreciative, and expansive thoughts in the present. Your ghosts will no longer be able to evoke guilt and fear by lamenting about what has happened or catastrophizing about what might. By living fully in the Now, you can find greater joy and fulfillment in your present circumstances, while allowing blessings to continue to flow in abundance.

When you surrender to each moment, and follow the path of greatest illumination, you will discover a synchronicity to life's events that seems almost magical in quality. People, places, and events line up perfectly in accordance with your fondest desires and highest aspirations. Although challenges continue to present themselves, life ceases to be a struggle.

Only your Inner Being can show you the way out of the darkness. Let it befriend you and guide you towards the life you have always wanted to live. The wonder of your inner panorama awaits your discovery and exploration.

PART I:
SPELLBOUND IN SHADOWLAND

CHAPTER ONE

RELATING SPELLS TO EARLY TRAUMAS

As was discussed in the introduction, while we are haunted by our history, we act as if we are bound by a spell that is outside our conscious awareness. I call this **spellbound behavior.** That spell compels us to repeat the same self-destructive patterns with the same distressing results. Our life becomes a reoccurring bad dream from which we cannot seem to awaken. This chapter describes the symptoms of spellbound behavior in greater detail, and outlines the relationship between our spellbound behavior and early traumas. By recognizing how our initial spell is cast, we can discover the most effective means of awakening from it. At the end of the chapter, you will have the opportunity to practice guided visualization—a process you can use throughout this book to break free of the past and transform your life in the present.

Spellbound Symptoms

Those who are being held captive by their past usually experience one or more of the following symptoms.

Low Self-Esteem

Spellbound individuals often report that they feel defective, worthless, and not good enough regardless of what they accomplish, and no matter what anyone tells them or they tell themselves. Many indicate that they feel like damaged goods. They frequently compare themselves to others, whom they rate as better-than or less-than themselves. They may have trouble valuing themselves, their time, and their needs and wants. Most say they have a hard time accepting that they deserve to have what they desire or to be happy.

Anxiety

Another typical characteristic is a pervasive feeling of anxiety that may or may not be associated with specific situations. At the extreme, a person may experience panic attacks or phobias. For example, one woman became so anxious in social situations that she became a prisoner of her own home, unable to leave even for brief periods without experiencing overwhelming terror accompanied by shortness of breath, lightheadedness, rapid heartbeat, increased perspiration, and the feeling that she was going to faint.

Depression

It is common for spellbound individuals to experience depression, even when there doesn't seem to be a justifiable reason in the present for feeling miserable. In fact, these people may become more uncomfortable when things are going well, as though they are waiting for the other shoe to fall at any time. Sometimes they report feeling more at ease with negative life occurrences than positive ones. It is not that they *want* bad things to happen, it is just that they *expect* bad things to happen and feel more comfortable dealing with disasters than blessings.

Negative Judgment

Many who are haunted by their past constantly remind themselves of how they should be thinking, feeling, or behaving. These "shoulds" are a way of mentally beating themselves up, and focusing on what is (ostensibly) wrong with them, rather than what is right. In addition, these people judge themselves severely and often by telling themselves things like "You're stupid, sick, crazy, ugly, fat, and unlovable." Other self-put-downs are words like "never" or "always," such as "You'll never amount to anything," or "You'll always be a failure," or "No one will ever love you." Frequently, those who judge themselves so negatively are also busy secretly judging others.

Self-Defeating Behaviors

It is also common for those who are spellbound to find themselves unconsciously sabotaging their own success or happiness by engaging in self-defeating behaviors. Frequently they repeat the same painful patterns in spite of every effort to stop. For example, one client had attended the same community college classes four terms in a row. Each term she would find a reason to drop the classes halfway through the semester. Another client had repeatedly lost his temper with his bosses and was fired from his last three jobs. One man had become emotionally involved with a number of women who lived far away from him, making it impossible to have the intimate relationship he desired.

Addictions

People who are spellbound find ways of deadening the pain of living. Some use alcohol or other drugs—both illegal and prescription—to block out painful feelings, while others overeat or overwork or try to use sex or romance to anaesthetize the hurt. Also common are addictions to gambling, spending, or speeding. For example, one woman told me she used overeating and shopping to unsuccessfully fill the big black hole inside her chest.

Psychosomatic Ailments

The emotional wounds we carry from the past can take their toll on us physically, resulting in such stress-related disorders as ulcers, headaches, colitis, and back pain. These ailments, which are most certainly real and potentially debilitating, are often exacerbated by our distressed emotional states. Sometimes, those with extensive early traumas will develop physical symptoms that cannot be fully explained by medical science. For example, one woman with a condition that baffled her physicians reported that she was allergic to natural light and would break out in hives when she spent just minutes out in the sun.

Abusive Behavior

Often, individuals who hurt others were victims of emotional and physical abuse in their own childhood. They may find it difficult to control their anger and therefore exhibit violent outbursts toward their mates, children, other people, or animals. For example, one man would have explosions during which he would scream obscenities at his family and punch holes in the walls and doors of their home with his fists.

Victimization

While some who were abused as children become violent adults, others continue to find themselves in situations where they are being physically, verbally, and/or sexually victimized. These people unconsciously seek out the same kinds of hurtful relationships in their adult lives that they experienced in their childhood. Some settle with mates who constantly berate and belittle them. Others may permit themselves to be repeatedly degraded, attacked, humiliated, or physically injured, and find it difficult to leave these dangerous and violent situations.

Paralysis

Many of those who are chained to the past find themselves governed by doubts and fears in the present. Even when a job, living situation, or relationship is hurting them or making them miserable, they find themselves paralyzed when it comes to making a change for the better. Though they may dream of writing a book, going back to school or learning to paint, they often lack the courage and confidence necessary to make these dreams a reality. Frequently even when their inner guidance is urging them to make a move in a new direction, they are terrified to take the first step, and discount their ability to chart the best course in life for themselves.

Avoidance of Intimacy

Sometimes the effects of being spellbound manifest as an avoidance of intimate relationships. In an effort to protect one's self from being hurt again, some people surround themselves with thick walls that prevent others from getting near them. While these folks may say they long for intimacy, they unconsciously do everything possible to keep others at a distance or to drive them away.

The Spell Is Cast During Early Traumas

These illusive figures that haunt us first cast their spell during an event or series of events that were traumatic for us. Traumatic incidents are painful episodes that leave a lasting impression. They may be unexpected and shocking. They may also be repeated and predictable occurrences we anticipated with silent dread. Examples of severe traumas include, but certainly are not limited to, the death or departure of a loved one; becoming ill; experiencing a natural disaster like an earthquake, hurricane, flood, or fire;

witnessing any form of violence or destruction; being emotionally, physically, and/or sexually abused; being neglected and/or abandoned by your caregivers; being the victim of prejudice or discrimination; being teased, humiliated, or rejected by caregivers, siblings or peers.

Traumas do not have to be severe to have a profound effect on your life. Attending a new school, getting braces on your teeth, being blamed by your parents for something you didn't do, missing the ball during an important game, or being laughed at for making a mistake in class are all incidents that could leave a lasting negative impression. Even watching a particularly frightening movie or television show at an impressionable age can have a traumatic effect on a child.

Because of differences in life experiences and personality characteristics, each of us may be traumatized by certain events that may not be remarkable or upsetting to someone else. Trauma is individually defined, and therefore personal. An unkind word may be easily ignored by one person and deeply wound another. A move to a new city might be an exciting adventure for one individual, and a tragic ending of many wonderful friendships for another.

It is more likely that we will be haunted by the traumas of our childhood and adolescence, than those of our adulthood. We are more vulnerable to the negative impact of distressful events in our childhood, because as children, we have fewer resources for dealing with painful life circumstances. The fewer the resources we have to cope with a painful event, the more likely it is to be traumatic for us. Thus, it usually takes more extreme circumstances to traumatize an adult than it does a child.

Certainly people can, and do, become traumatized in their adult years. Some events, such as war, are so devastating that even adult survivors may find themselves reliving the horrors for decades. However, barring such life-shattering circumstances in our later years, most of us will discover that the phantoms moved in and made themselves at home in the shadows of our consciousness long before the challenging events of our adulthood.

The Casting of the Spell

We fall under the spell of our ghosts during the distressful moments of our lives when we experience an unpleasant or unbearable situation in which we are flooded with strong emotions that cannot be expressed; feel powerless; make limiting decisions; lose parts of ourselves; and, become fixated in our personal development. Each of these components of an original trauma is discussed below.

Traumas Induce Strong Emotions

Since traumatic events are painful, frightening, and overwhelming, it is normal for them to activate a flood of intense, unpleasant feelings. During traumas we are usually deluged with a range of emotions, which may include: shame, anger, terror, rage, guilt, hate, frustration, and grief. In ideal circumstances, we would have the opportunity to release these emotions freely without impairment. Unfortunately, as children and adolescents, and even at times as adults, we are more likely to be blocked in expressing what we feel.

Why are we often blocked from expressing the intense emotions triggered by a traumatic event? First, it may be unsafe to express feelings, as in the case of a child who is being abused by an adult. The child knows that saying how he or she feels means risking further harm. In some situations, it can even be life threatening for the victim to speak up. A second factor is that children rarely have the language to express what they are feeling during or after a painful and confusing incident. Even when given the opportunity to vent emotions, children often have difficulty expressing their feelings. A third reason is that well-meaning adults may discourage a child from expressing negative feelings by saying things like "Be brave, don't cry," or "You shouldn't be afraid." Children may get the message that it is not okay for them to feel whatever they may be feeling. Fourth, children often try to "protect" their caregivers by not speaking out about their experiences. And last, these events often induce shock, which causes children to become disconnected from their emotions during the event and for some time afterward. While this is nature's coping mechanism, it does not make the bad feelings go away—it only makes it possible for us to survive a tragedy without falling apart at the time. We may be fooled into thinking that our numbness means we don't have any strong feelings about the catastrophic event. But actually, the numbness is like an anesthetic that protects us from pain that may be too much to endure at the time. Some of us become addicted to such a psychological painkiller and go through decades of our lives numbing ourselves to the awareness of feelings that remain unresolved.

Intense, unexpressed emotions do not go away. Rather, they lie buried in the dark places within us, haunting us with living nightmares. Until we make peace with our past, we may find ourselves in situations that activate those original feelings over and over again.

Traumas Evoke Feelings of Powerlessness

It is natural for us to feel powerless during traumatic events. Whether we are confronted with a natural disaster, the death of a

16

sibling, a criminal assault, or the wrath of a raging parent, we are generally in a helpless position to stop the dreaded event from taking place. Our frustration and suffering are intensified during such an ordeal due to our complete lack of control over what is happening to us or to those we love. We are left feeling totally vulnerable and incapable of protecting ourselves or others. Often, powerlessness and victimization become a central theme in our life script. We may play the role of either the perpetrator or the victim until we awaken from our spell and reclaim our personal power in the present.

Traumas Cause Us to Make Limiting Decisions

During original traumas we are especially likely to make limiting decisions about ourselves and our lives. For example, we may decide that people we love will always hurt or leave us, or that the world is an unsafe place. It is common for children who are mistreated by their caregivers to blame themselves and decide that they are bad or unlovable and that they deserve to suffer. For example, throughout his childhood Jason was routinely beaten by his father. Accompanying the physical abuse were reminders from his father that he was a "stupid idiot who would never amount to anything." Like most abused children, Jason grew up believing that he deserved the horrible beatings he received from his father, and that he is fundamentally bad. He also decided that he is stupid, worthless, and unlovable. Jason believed his father's words, spoken in rage, and took them as the absolute truth about himself. As an adolescent, Jason became addicted to drugs and ended up in a juvenile detention facility. In adulthood, Jason is lonely, suicidal, and battling alcoholism. Jason's belief that he is bad and unworthy continues to play a central role in his life drama.

Like Jason, each of us spends our early years making and rein-forcing many important decisions about ourselves, life in general, and other people. For example, we decide if others can be trusted; what our capabilities are; what our shortcomings are; and what we deserve in life. We formulate these judgments primarily based on our life experiences, how we are treated and what happened to us, as well as through observations we make about the important peo-ple in our lives, and what we are taught by family members, teach-ers, and friends. These decisions lead to habitual ways of thinking that we may automatically revert to throughout our lives—unless we make a conscious effort to entertain different thoughts.

We use our early decisions to formulate our expectations. Some limiting decisions we make during traumas may haunt us throughout our lives in the form of negative expectations. Once we have decided to expect the worst from ourselves and others, then it is only a matter of watching our negative drama unfold in just the way we have unwittingly set it up to be. Sadly, most of us consider our unfulfilling life experiences to be evidence that our negative expectations are indeed correct. We do not recognize that simply by altering our way of thinking, we can rewrite our life script so we get what we really want in life, rather than what we don't want.

During Traumas We May Become Disconnected from Parts of Ourselves

During traumatic episodes we may also become disconnected from positive aspects of ourselves. It is not that these disconnected parts are gone forever, it is that we have temporarily lost the ability to access them. What are these missing parts? It depends upon the kind of trauma, and the person who experiences it. Victims of sex-ual abuse may temporarily lose their ability to find pleasure in sexuality. Those who experience natural disasters like floods or hurricanes may misplace their sense of security and stability. Those who are the target of prejudice and discrimination may lose sight of their trust and faith in others. Depending upon the situation, we may lose touch with such qualities as courage, determination, the ability to love, playfulness, inner peace, or self-confidence. Naturally, it is also possible for us to find new inner resources during traumatic episodes. Sometimes it is in surviving such painful circumstances that we discover a previously hidden strength!

We May Become Fixated During Traumas

Still another of the effects of trauma is that a part of us may become stuck or fixated at the moment when the painful event occurs. Thus, as adults we may end up behaving in certain situations in the same way that we behaved when we were children. Most often these responses are unsatisfying in the results they produce. Typically, the situations that trigger our childlike response pattern tend to be those that resemble the original traumas in some way. For example, George reported that when his boss would get angry with him, he would feel like he was a bad little boy again, in danger of being yelled at by his raging mother. George's response to this situation was to feel terrified, to say nothing in his own defense, and to avoid being around his boss whenever possible. Not surprisingly, these were the same actions George would take to protect himself from the wrath of his mother. In cases of more extreme trauma, I have seen individuals whose fixation at an early stage of development was so complete that during times of trauma the person looked, spoke, and behaved like a child or adolescent despite being thirty, forty, or fifty years old.

Once we have been traumatized, it is natural to do what we can to avoid suffering the same way again. This means calling up our psychological defenses. The problem is that we may continue to use defensive tactics long after they have become maladaptive. While we are fixated at an earlier stage of development, we are on "automatic pilot," clinging to the coping strategies of our childhood even though they are now counterproductive. For example, Josie was in a military family that frequently moved. After having to leave dear friends behind several times, Josie learned to protect herself from such losses by not letting anyone get too close to her. As an adult, Josie is lonely with few close relationships. The walls she erected as a child are still there, although the circumstances of her life have changed considerably. In her efforts to keep herself from experiencing the pain of loss, she has also shut out the joys of love and intimacy. Josie is not conscious of her walls and doesn't understand why she has such difficulty making friends. Her spell shrouds her in a fog, preventing her from recognizing the ways in which she perpetuates her loneliness.

Not everyone employs the same defensive tactics given the same stressful circumstances. People of different personality types often reveal a preference for utilizing different kinds of psychological protection. I suggest that those readers who are interested in learning more about the relationship between personality and defenses read my book *Survival Games Personalities Play* (SunInk Publications, 1992) in which I address this topic in detail.

The Past That Binds You

So how do the ghosts from the past keep you spellbound? By compelling you to unconsciously choose those situations that enable you to experience the same feelings that were triggered by the initial trauma; re-experience a sense of helplessness, powerlessness, or victimization; reinforce limiting decisions; remain disconnected from certain parts of yourself; and, remain stuck or fixated at an earlier stage of development, the shadows of your past continue to darken your future.

We can summarize the characteristics of spellbound behavior with the following chart:

During the Initial Trauma a Person Will:	In the Present Situation the One Who Is Spellbound Will:
1. Feel strong emotions	1. Re-experience the same emotions
2. Feel like a powerless victim	2. Feel like a powerless victim
3. Make limiting decisions	3. Reinforce those limiting decisions
4. Lose parts of the self	4. Remain disconnected from parts of the self
5. Become fixated at the age when the initial trauma occurred	5. Feel and behave as if at the age when the initial trauma occurred

Charlotte's Spellbound Behavior

Charlotte was sexually abused by her father during her childhood and adolescence. As an adult, she finds herself only attracted to married men—often with the same first name as her father. Although she longs for a loving partnership, she engages in one painful affair after another with married men who use and abuse her. Let us examine Charlotte's spellbound behavior using the model presented above.

Each time Charlotte has an affair with a married man she feels the tremendous shame and self-disgust she originally felt when her father abused her. The secretive nature of each affair and fear of exposure are also familiar to her. Charlotte's father had threatened to kill her dog if she told anyone what he was doing to her.

Charlotte also revisits the experience of helplessness, hopelessness, and powerlessness she felt during her childhood abuse each time a boyfriend mistreats her. Thus, she continues to play the role of victim in her life story.

In addition, Charlotte's affairs remind her that she really is unlovable and unworthy, and that men she loves will always hurt her. While spellbound, she does not think to question the validity of the limiting attitudes and habitual thoughts that keep her imprisoned in her own personal hell.

Throughout the replaying of this painful scenario, Charlotte remains cut off from her powerful, capable, confident adult self, devoid of self-esteem and self-respect. Hence, the very qualities that Charlotte needs to maintain a satisfying intimate partnership seem inaccessible to her.

Charlotte reverts to feeling and behaving like a dependent and needy adolescent in response to her boyfriends' actions. Though she is aware that her actions are not getting her what she really wants, she has been unable to break the pattern. She remains a teenage girl in a woman's body.

When Charlotte's father molested her, she learned to turn off her sexual feelings and physical sensations in order to survive those painful scenes. Charlotte still finds that she becomes numb and feels as though she is disconnected from her body when engaging in sexual activities. In each new relationship she is disappointed when she is unable to feel physical pleasure during sex. Although the survival tactics of childhood are no longer necessary, she has yet to release them in adulthood.

While we have been focusing on Charlotte, it is also important to note that each of Charlotte's married boyfriends is probably grappling with his own unresolved past. It is common for those who are spellbound to be attracted to one another. And each is likely to behave in ways that revisit the others' most painful traumas. I would guess that several of Charlotte's boyfriends grew up watching one or both of their parents have affairs. Thus, in finding Charlotte, these men recreate a familiar scenario from their own childhood.

Using Exercises to Awaken from Your Spell

Awakening from your spellbound state means stepping out of the shadows and into the light. When you rouse yourself from your trance, you dissolve the inner distortions, deceptions, and lies that have blinded you from seeing the truth of who you are. As you part the veils of illusion, you are able to recognize and choose a path of greater happiness and fulfillment.

This book will guide you through a series of 21 exercises you can use to leave the past behind and awaken to your true nature. I suggest you begin right now by doing the exercise that follows. Exercise #1, entitled "Creating Your Heart Sanctuary" will help to familiarize you with the experience of guided visualization, which is used in many of the other 20 processes you will find throughout this book. Guided visualization is a technique that combines deep relaxation with mental imagery to provide a means of accessing your inner guidance and creative imagination.

Visualization

When you are doing the guided visualization exercises it is helpful to be playful with your imagination and to be willing to *pretend*. There is no one right way to visualize. However you do it is the right way for you. Involve as many of your senses as you can in your mental imagery, and don't be concerned if you don't get a clear picture. Some people see things more clearly in their mind's eye, others feel, smell, or hear more clearly.

Distracting Voice

There may be a little voice in the back of your head during the visualization telling you that you are not doing it correctly. The voice may also try to distract you by reminding you of all of the things on your "to do" list. You can use that voice as a signal to refocus on the imagery. Continue to gently bring your attention back to the guided meditation as often as is necessary. Eventually the voice will go away.

Practice

I suggest you take some time now to practice focusing your attention inward and attaining a state of deep relaxation by using the following exercise. The more you practice using guided imagery, the easier it will become.

For this guided visualization and others that follow in later chapters, you can either memorize each exercise beforehand, have someone read it to you very slowly, or record yourself reading it on a tape which you can then play back to do the process. This exercise and many that follow are also available on a set of compact discs, entitled: *Guided Visualizations for Breaking the Spell of the Past and Entering the Joyous Now.* Ordering information is located in the back of this book.

You will also find a list of suggested music at the end of this book, which you can play in the background to help you relax while you do the guided meditations.

In this exercise, you will create a heart sanctuary, which you will use during future guided visualizations for awakening from your spellbound state.

Exercise #1
Creating Your Heart Sanctuary

1. Find a comfortable place where you can be alone and quiet for fifteen minutes. Choose a position (sitting or lying down) that allows you to keep your spine straight and to relax without falling asleep. You may wish to play soft, soothing music in the background while you do this exercise.

2. Close your eyes and begin taking long, slow, deep breaths. Give yourself plenty of time for every breath. Notice the rising and falling of the area below your navel as you inhale and exhale. Keeping your eyes closed, you may gently roll your eyes upward if it is comfortable for you. For some, this enhances the process of relaxation. Imagine that you are inhaling peace, up through the soles of your feet. Every time you exhale, feel yourself letting go of all tension, just letting it drain away. Breathe relaxation into any part of your body that needs to relax more deeply and completely. Feel your body responding by becoming more and more relaxed, surrendering to the serenity and comfort of this

moment. Notice your mind becoming as calm and clear as a deep, blue sky on a cloudless summer day. Give yourself permission to take this mini-vacation, as you begin to access the deepest and most peaceful part of your being.

3. Now imagine that the area around your heart is easily opening up and expanding until you become aware of a special doorway. The doorway leads directly into your heart sanctuary—a place that is completely safe, peaceful, nurturing, and loving. It may resemble a favorite place you visited in the past, or someplace you have just created in your mind's eye. In this setting, you can access your unlimited potential for creativity, inner guidance, self-transformation, and self-healing. Everything about your heart sanctuary is exactly as you want it to be. Use all of your senses now to imagine exactly how it looks, smells, feels, and sounds here in your heart sanctuary. Notice the intense colors and interesting textures. Does it smell salty, sweet, musky, or like pine? Do you feel a gentle wind blowing? Is the temperature cool or warm, moist or dry? Do you hear music, a babbling brook, the sound of birds singing, or the leaves rustling in the wind? Notice that the air you breathe here is composed of tiny droplets of peace. Feel every level of your being becoming saturated with the serenity and love that are so abundantly available here.

4. Spend as much time as you like exploring your heart sanctuary. Become aware of how good you feel just being here—safe and serene, calm and comfortable, peaceful and protected.

5. When you are ready to return to the room, tell yourself that you are coming back feeling clear-headed, refreshed, and alert. Open your eyes, stretch, and feel yourself returning fully and completely to the present moment.

You will often be asked to return to your heart sanctuary as a starting point for future exercises in this book. Practice visiting your heart sanctuary daily, until you can easily and effortlessly imagine yourself there.

CHAPTER TWO
RECOGNIZING SPELLBOUND PATTERNS

In order to awaken from the trance that holds you captive, it is important to become conscious of your current spellbound behavior. Even as you begin to shine the light of awareness on your self-sabotaging reactions to life's circumstances, you are activating positive changes; the ghosts from your past can only control you when hiding in the dark recesses of your psyche.

Fortunately, it is easy to discover the ways in which you are imprisoned by your past if you begin to pay close attention to your feelings and your thoughts. Life has a wonderful way of letting us know where we are most in need of healing, by putting people and events in our path that are likely to trigger our most unhealthy reactions: These relationships and situations spotlight the parts of us which are in need of greater light. They are an invitation for personal growth, gifts in the form of contentious co-workers or difficult family members who help us identify when we are under the spell of the past. The people and circumstances causing us the greatest distress can be of great value, if we observe carefully what they evoke within us. Our emotional reactions, physical sensations, and negative thoughts reveal exactly where we are held captive by our history, and how we can cut the ties to the past that bind us.

Look for Emotional Over-Reactions

Pay particular attention to intense, overwhelming, emotional reactions to current life situations that are distressing, but not devastating. While our rational mind may say, "Certainly this situation is upsetting, but it is not the end of the world," we can't stop ourselves from feeling as if it really *is* the end of the world. An event that should be a minor source of frustration ignites our rage; or, we respond to a somewhat stressful circumstance with terror or panic.

These seemingly out-of-control emotional reactions are accompanied by physical sensations, which we often do not recognize until we tune into our bodies and ask ourselves what we are sensing at the time. How does our abdomen feel? What sensations do we feel in our chest, in our head, neck and shoulders, or in our legs and arms? Typically, each pattern of emotional reactivity is paired for a particular individual with certain distinguishable physical sensations. This means we can learn to identify how it feels in our bodies as we are in the grips of anxiety, anger, fear, jealousy, or whatever emotion has managed to take us over. These physical sensations can be used to identify that aspect of our past that is ruling us in the present. Part two of this book will show you how to use this information to awaken from your ghost-induced trance.

What follows is an example of how one woman's extreme emotional reaction and its physical concomitants were used to detect a remnant of her past that had been haunting her for fifty-five years, and how this discovery enabled her to set herself free.

A Grandmother Meets Her Ghosts

Carol, a dynamic, sixty-three-year-old grandmother, was surprised at her reaction to the divorce of her daughter and son-in-law. She found herself weeping uncontrollably at the thought that her seven-year-old granddaughter, Brittany, "wouldn't have her father anymore." Carol was so upset about Brittany "losing her father" that she was unable to sleep at night, or enjoy her usually active life.

30

During our therapy session, as Carol told me about her concerns, it struck me as odd that she should be so emotionally distraught over Brittany's loss of her father. After all, Brittany's father was going to be living around the corner from his ex-wife, and Brittany would be living with him half of the time. I also found it interesting that Carol was not nearly as upset about her four-year-old grandson's loss of his father, although she was very close to the boy. These clues led me to suspect that Carol was under the spell of ghosts from her past.

I asked Carol to close her eyes, become relaxed, and focus on the feelings she was having *in her body* about Brittany losing her father. Carol identified a nauseous feeling in her stomach, a tightening in her throat, a sharp feeling in her chest, and a swirling feeling in her head. Then, while keeping her eyes closed, I asked Carol to go back to a time in her childhood or adolescence when she felt the same feelings in her body. Carol began to sob uncontrollably, as she recalled having the same feelings in her body as a seven-year-old when she learned that her father had been killed in an auto accident. She continued to cry deeply over the death of her father. Through her tears she explained that at the time of his death, everyone told her to be strong for her mother. Being strong meant shedding no tears. There in my office, fifty-six years after his death, Carol cried *for the first time in her life* over the death of her father. And it was her granddaughter's "loss of her father" that reminded her of her own loss at the same age.

In addition to witnessing her grief, I guided Carol in finding and nurturing the seven-year-old child inside of her. That child had been waiting for a long time to hear that she didn't have to be strong for anyone, and that it was okay for her to express her sadness.

The next time I saw Carol she reported that she was feeling significantly better. Although she was sad that Brittany's parents were divorcing, she no longer felt overwhelmed with grief over the event. She was sleeping soundly at night and enjoying life again. Carol had healed wounds she had been carrying for over half of a century by shining the light of present awareness into the dark spaces within.

Our Phantoms Affect Our Primary Relationships

Typically, patterns of emotional over-reaction are apparent in our relationships with our spouses. Unconsciously, we select partners who behave in ways that activate our spellbound reactions. This means that our most intimate relationships are often our most challenging, and that they also provide the greatest opportunity for personal growth. Our life partners are likely to be helping us become aware of any unfinished business from the past that is ruling our lives in the present. For example, Ted is preoccupied with his work and frequently spends long hours at the office. Susan is hurt and angry and feels unloved because Ted works so much. When she begs him to spend more time with her, Ted feels Susan is being bossy and over-controlling, and he concludes that nothing he does will ever be good enough for her. His response is to physically and emotionally withdraw from Susan. This makes Susan feel even more unloved, and she tries even harder to get him to open up to her.

What does this relationship pattern have to do with Susan and Ted's past? For Susan, Ted's long work hours trigger reminders of her father's absence from her life. Susan's parents divorced when she was little, and she always felt that her father's infrequent appearances in her life meant he didn't love her. Hence, she over-reacts to Ted's excessive working with feelings of being neglected and unloved. Her outbursts mirror the way her mother treated her father. For Ted, Susan's reactions are reminders of his smothering

32

and over-controlling mother. Ted's withdrawal from Susan is the same defense he used to deal with his mother's intrusiveness. Susan's eruptions are also reminiscent of his father's disapproval of him—hence the irrational conclusion that nothing he does will ever be good enough for Susan.

Ted and Susan are stuck because their negative trances color their perceptions and expectations of their partner's behavior and control their reactions. This keeps them repeating a familiar but unsatisfying relationship cycle. As Ted and Susan deal with their own phantoms, they will be free to see their partner's behavior through clear lenses, to hold more positive expectations, and to respond in new and more creative ways.

We Take Our Ghosts to Work with Us

It is not just in our home lives that our emotional reactions may be affected by unresolved traumas. In my consulting work with corporations, I have seen many examples of how painful experiences from the past can color and distort an employee's relationships with colleagues. For example, Don is extremely jealous of the attention given to his co-worker, Mark, who has been recognized for being an outstanding performer on the company's sales team. The more attention Mark receives for his accomplishments, the more inadequate Don feels. He avoids all contact with Mark and privately tries to sabotage Mark's success whenever possible. Don's reaction to Mark is due, in part, to the old wounds he carries in relation to his family of origin. Don's brother, Kevin, was the star quarterback on the high school football team. Don was uncoordinated and overweight, and intensely jealous of his brother. He deeply resented the attention his brother received at home and at school. Don felt that his parents, teachers, and peers valued his brother more than they valued him. Whether or not this is true is irrelevant. What does matter is that these are the feelings Don carries within him. One way for Don to stop reacting negatively to Mark's successes is for him to deal with the old feelings he holds regarding his perceived lack of self worth. Until he does this, he will continue to find himself in situations where his jealousy and inadequacy buttons are being pushed.

About the Exercises in This Chapter

The two exercises in this chapter are meant to help you recognize the ghosts from the past that are controlling your life in the present. This means they are designed to help you recall your *subjective* memories for the purpose of healing yourself. At times, your *subjective* memory may be different from *objective* reality. It is important to avoid confusing one with the other. For example, you may remember being run over by a white truck, but the police detective determined that it was a blue van that actually hit you. Fortunately, to release the past and move on with your life, it is not necessary to establish what really happened during the traumatic event. Often it is not possible to find corroborating data to let you know if what you remember really occurred or not. While these exercises are not designed to help you establish what actually happened to you, they can help you locate those subjective memories or memory fragments that are holding you captive in the present. In part two, you will be guided in using this information to set yourself free.

In the following exercise you can use your present emotional triggers and physical responses to locate any unresolved traumas that require your attention.

Exercise #2
Using Emotional Triggers and Physical Sensations to Locate Unresolved Traumas

1. Close your eyes, take a few deep breaths, and imagine yourself once again in your heart sanctuary (as described in exercise one). Reassure yourself that you can immediately return to the comfort and safety of your heart sanctuary if you are feeling anxious or distressed at any time during this exercise.

2. Once you are feeling calm and comfortable, think of a situation in your present life that triggers an emotional or physical reaction within you—perhaps stronger than you would reasonably expect under the circumstances. You may even tell yourself that you shouldn't be so upset, but you are unable to get your emotions under control. You may feel angry, depressed, scared, anxious, resentful, jealous, hurt, or any other strong emotion.

3. As you focus on the emotions and physical sensations you are experiencing in the situation you have identified, notice in greater detail what you are feeling in your body. Where are you feeling the emotions in your body, and how do they feel? What are the physical sensations you are having in your body and what do they feel like? Describe how your body feels in as much detail as possible. For example, notice if any parts of your body feel hot, cold,

light, heavy, tight, loose, burning, tingling, aching, nauseous, swirling, or empty. If you notice how your stomach feels, ask yourself how your chest, back, legs, head, and neck feel. Scan as much of your body as you can.

4. Now go back to another time during the last ten years when you felt the same feelings. Stay with the feelings in your body, and let your mind show you another time when you felt the same way. When a scene comes to mind, notice where you are, what is happening, and how you are feeling in the scene. See if you can estimate your age at the time. Write down what you observe during this process.

5. Now go through the same process again, going back another ten years. Repeat the process until you have gone all the way back to before the age of ten.

6. Return to your heart sanctuary one last time to reconnect with the peace and comfort there, allowing yourself to linger for as long as you like before opening your eyes and coming back to the present.

7. Chances are good that many or all of the scenes you recalled during this exercise represent unresolved traumas for you. Please keep your notes from this exercise for use in part two of this book.

Common Thought Traps
among Those Who Are Spellbound

Another way to locate the shadowy figures hiding in your base-
ment is to examine your beliefs. There are certain negative patterns of thought, which I have found to be dominant among
individuals who are haunted by their past. I call these "thought
traps," because they are often the means by which we remain
imprisoned in lives of misery and pain.

Although we are focused here on the negative thought patterns
you may keep activating, remember that you also have
many positive thoughts—both about those aspects of your life in
which you experience joy, success, and fulfillment, as well as those
aspects of your life in which you are currently experiencing distress.

As you review the list, it may help to keep in mind that you
can train yourself to avoid thought traps, even those you have
been getting stuck in for decades. Just decide you are going to
catch yourself whenever you fall into one of the traps, and choose
to think something else instead. A thought trap can only hurt you
if you are snared by it. As long as you avoid stepping into a particular thought trap, it has no negative impact on your life. Since
it often takes some practice to change old habits of thought, chapter five offers practical tips on how to establish ways of thinking
which are more life-enhancing. Ten common thought traps are
described below.

Thought Trap #1
"I am unworthy."

During early traumas it is common for us to decide that we are to
blame for whatever bad thing is happening to us. Children blame

themselves for the death of a family member, a car accident, or their parents' divorce. I have treated many men and women who were physically and/or sexually abused in childhood, and all of them blame themselves for their abuse. I have even had clients who blame themselves for not having protected a brother or sister from being beaten by a drunken parent.

When we believe we are to blame for some horrible thing that befalls us, we ultimately decide we must be bad. And because we believe we are bad, we decide that we do not deserve good things like love, joy, success, prosperity, good health, peace of mind, or a fulfilling life. We may want these things more than anything in the world; however, we do not allow ourselves to have them because we believe we are unworthy of them.

For example, if you think you are unworthy of love, you will make certain that you do not allow yourself to receive love in your life. Love can be knocking at your door, but you will either not hear it, or lock the door and run the other way. You may even unconsciously seek out relationships in which it is guaranteed that love is not part of the equation. This is because *we only allow ourselves to have what we believe we truly deserve in our lives.*

The message that you are unworthy is the biggest lie the ghosts will ever tell you. It is the very opposite of the truth. You are worthy of the best that life has to offer, no matter who you are, no matter what you have or haven't accomplished in your life. The minute you start thinking you are worthy is the minute your life will begin to change in amazing ways, and you will receive greater blessings than you ever imagined. The choice is yours—accept your inherent worthiness or continue to believe the big lie that you don't deserve to have what you want.

Thought Trap #2
"I am not good enough."

Your ghosts are only too happy to remind you of your supposed personal inadequacies. As long as you are haunted, you are likely to hear your tormentors reminding you that you are *not* okay—and sadly, you are likely to believe them. Inner phantoms are often masterful in comparing us to others, and reminding us that we fall short in the comparison. They know our greatest insecurities and capitalize on them. They focus on whatever perceived inadequacies bother us the most—physical, mental, professional, academic, or social. They ignore your strengths, and minimize your accomplishments. No matter what you do, they are always happy to remind you that you are just not good enough.

People who believe they aren't good enough go through their lives with inferiority complexes; they don't believe in themselves, and they don't expect others to believe in them either. They may avoid taking risks and meeting life's challenges, since they are insecure and lack confidence. Or, they may be over-achievers, always trying to prove to themselves and to others that they really do have value. But typically, despite their numerous achievements on the outside, they continue to feel worthless and inadequate on the inside.

Your phantoms can only convince you that you are less than others if you play the comparison game. Your willingness to compare yourself with others gives them the power to make you feel inadequate, and becomes an excuse for not stepping out of your comfort zone.

And yet, you are not alive to win a contest at being the smartest, fastest, richest, thinnest, or most talented. You are here to express your uniqueness, to create the life that you desire and to find the richness and perfection of each moment. These things can only happen when you throw away your yardstick, and start appreciating your own beauty and the beauty of others.

Thought Trap #3
"It is essential that others approve of me."

People who have decided they aren't good enough *and* that they aren't worthy sometimes conclude that their only value comes from keeping other people happy. When we are emotionally abused as children, we may long for the approval we did not receive in childhood, and become overly dependent upon receiving it in adulthood. While it is wonderful to take pleasure in the happiness of others, these individuals are *desperate* for the acceptance of others. They will sacrifice their health, peace of mind, and even their personal integrity to avoid the disapproval of others. Often people with these codependent patterns were neglected or given the role of parental caretaker early in their childhood.

Certainly, it is nice when we have the approval of others. But when we spend our lives doing only those things that please others, chances are we won't take the path that is right for us, for fear of others' disapproval. We make others the authority regarding our own lives, and allow their voices to drown out the voice of our own inner guidance. And what do we do when two or more important people in our lives disagree about what is best for us?

Only you know where you need to go and how you need to get there. Realize that it is impossible to have everyone's sanction for everything you do. There is great freedom in being comfortable with the disapproval of others. The freedom to be yourself. The freedom to follow your dreams. The freedom to express your uniqueness in the world. The freedom to pursue whatever makes you happy. The freedom to create. The freedom to thrive in this lifetime.

Thought Trap #4
"I am powerless."

Because of the feeling of powerlessness that typically accompanies trauma, we often decide that we have absolutely no control over what happens to us in life. The person who falls into this thought trap plays the role of helpless victim in his or her life drama. This individual consistently makes choices that have negative consequences, but he or she feels like a hopeless victim of life's circumstances. When opportunities for change present themselves, these folks look the other way. People with this habit of thought are rarely proactive in their lives, and tend to blame other people or circumstances outside of themselves for their unhappiness. As a result, they consistently feel powerless to create positive change in their lives.

When you free yourself from this thought trap, you step out of the role of victim and into the role of writer, director, and star performer in your own life drama. Rather than feeling angry and resentful about your life story as it has unfolded, you begin to deliberately fashion a new script that matches your deepest longings and fondest desires.

Thought Trap #5
"I cannot trust myself."

When we take responsibility for the bad things that happened to us in childhood, we often come to the conclusion that we just can't trust ourselves to make good choices in life. If you don't trust yourself, then you are likely to look to other people to tell you how to live your life. Rather than being your own authority, you make other people the experts regarding what is best for you. You end up rejecting your most reliable source of guidance—your own inner advisor.

People who don't trust themselves sometimes avoid making decisions entirely. For example, they will avoid getting involved in an intimate relationship because they fear they will either select the wrong partner, or mistakenly do something to destroy the relationship if they do find the right partner. Similarly, they may avoid leaving a job they hate because they don't trust themselves to find and follow a more fulfilling career path. Although their inner guidance may be screaming at them to take a certain action, they don't do it because they doubt their ability to know what is best for them.

You do know the best path for you. And it is only when you begin to trust yourself that your life will be what you truly want it to be. Instead of developing increasing tolerance for being miserable where you are, step out of your comfort zone and follow your inner urgings in the direction of a better life.

Thought Trap #6
"I cannot trust other people."

Often early trauma involves other people who neglect or mistreat us in some way. And too often those who abused or neglected us are the people we completely depended upon for our survival—our parents and other caregivers. When this happens, we are left to conclude that it is not safe to trust people. A variation of this belief is that people we love will always disappoint or hurt us. After all, if you can't rely on those entrusted with your care, who can you trust?

If you think you cannot trust people, or that those you love will always hurt you, then the best way to protect yourself is to avoid getting close to others. You may erect walls to isolate yourself from others and maintain plenty of emotional distance, push people who care for you away by getting angry or abusive when

42

they are loving, or provoke others until they finally do what you expect them to do—walk away without looking back.

When we assume everyone will behave as our abusers did, we fail to recognize all of the kind and gentle people in our world. There is much to be gained from removing walls, appreciating the good in others, and letting love in.

Thought Trap #7
"There is not enough."

People who have experienced lack during their early lives often carry that expectation into their adult years; whatever it is they lacked as children, they expect to lack as adults. For example, if there was not enough money to meet their basic needs as children, they do not expect to have enough in adulthood. Thus, if you grew up in poverty, it may be difficult for you to imagine yourself as a prosperous adult. You may find that even when you do have plenty, you experience a looming fear that your abundance is only temporary and likely to be taken away at any moment.

People who fear there is not enough tend to be worriers. They worry that even though they have enough money, love, success, joy, or good health today, they may lose it tomorrow. The "lack mentality" says that there is never enough of what I want or need. Because of the self-fulfilling prophecy, those who decide there isn't enough tend to experience real deprivation in their lives: They expect to be impoverished, and so they are. Whether they had a lack of financial abundance, love, success, freedom, or joy—their adult lives often continue to be deficient in whatever was missing in their painful childhoods.

You experience lack primarily because you expect things to be that way. And, as you reverse your negative expectations to anticipate abundance rather than scarcity, you will discover that there is an unlimited supply of whatever you desire.

Thought Trap #8
"Life is a struggle."

When we have had to struggle to survive the ordeals of our early years, it is common for us to conclude that struggle is an integral part of life. Once we have decided that life is a struggle, we tend to make everything harder than it needs to be. We expect it to be difficult to accomplish our goals, and so it is. It does not occur to us to think of ways to make things easier on ourselves because we accept struggle as a way of life. Of course, many objectives require dedication and hard work. However, a belief in the necessity of struggle means it has to hurt to be worthwhile. It means we may not even recognize that there is an easier path to follow. And even if we see it, we won't choose the joyful path when there is a painful alternative.

Why continue to make it difficult for yourself? You can decide to let go of struggle, and to allow the process of attaining your goals to be joyful for you. Things can be much easier, if you let them.

Thought Trap #9
"It is not safe for me to be myself."

Often during traumatic events we decide that it is not safe for us to be ourselves, and that we must hide our true nature. So we put on masks to disguise our true selves, our genuine thoughts, feelings, and desires. We believe that revealing them will cause us more pain, and decide that it is better to pretend to be something we are not, rather than to risk rejection and ridicule for being ourselves. We learn to put on a smile when we are feeling sad, and to swallow our truths and speak convincing lies. Sometimes we become so accustomed to our masks, we forget they are merely a false front that we use to protect ourselves from hurt. Eventually many of us become alienated from the real person hiding behind the disguise. We lose contact with our inner truth and wisdom, and wonder why we feel so depressed and unfulfilled in our lives.

There is nothing more satisfying than expressing your individuality in the world. When you remove the mask you hide behind, some may disapprove of who you are, but many others will be drawn to your genuine nature and strong sense of self.

Thought Trap #10
"I am responsible for everyone else's happiness."

During a traumatic childhood, we may come to believe that it is our job to keep everyone else happy. We may have received this message directly from parents who needed us to take care of them and our siblings, or we may have discovered at an early age that the role of caretaker helped us to solicit love and acceptance from others. We become masterful at fostering dependency in others. "As long as they need me, they certainly won't leave me." The problem is, that in trying to keep everyone else happy (which is of course, an impossible task) we end up sacrificing our own joy and well-being. When everyone else's needs come first, our own needs are ignored. Over time, this is a perfect set-up for depression or physical disorders. We can only neglect ourselves for so long, before our bodies, emotions, and Spirit, let us know that our lives are severely out of balance.

There is a difference between caring for others and being responsible for their happiness. While it is wonderful to give from your heart to those you care about, each of us is ultimately responsible for our own happiness and well-being. Set others free to find

45

this for themselves, and turn your attention to taking good care of you. By maintaining your own mental, emotional, and physical health, you will have more to give in the end. Learn to replenish your own cup first, and then help others to do the same.

You Can Use Limiting Beliefs to Locate Your Phantoms

Exercise three shows you how to use your most familiar thought traps in order to locate the ghosts that are controlling your life in the present.

Exercise #3
Using Thought Traps to Locate Unresolved Traumas

1. Ask yourself to identify one thought trap that snares you more than others. It may be on the preceding list of ten thought traps, or it may be something completely different that occurs to you. One way to identify your negative thought patterns is to look at an area of your life that is not working for you. Ask yourself what beliefs would be in alignment with what your life looks like today. Remember that beliefs are different from desires. You may *want* something very badly, but *believe* deep down that you don't deserve to have it, or that it isn't possible.

2. Close your eyes, breathe deeply, relax, and imagine you are back in your heart sanctuary. Feel the safe-

ty and the comfort of being there. Tell yourself that you can return to your heart sanctuary any time during this exercise if you are feeling anxious or distressed.

3. Now ask your mind to take you back to the first time you decided things must be this way. For example, ask your mind to go back to when you first decided that you don't deserve to have what you want. When the scene appears to you, notice everything you can about it. Where are you, how old are you, what are you feeling, and what is happening? Get more clarity about the decision you are making at that moment.

4. Moving on, ask your self to locate other scenes in which that first decision was reinforced or strengthened. Take note of each additional scene, asking yourself again where you are, how old you are, what you are feeling, and what is happening. Notice also how you are strengthening or reinforcing your earlier decision.

5. Return to your heart sanctuary for as long as you like to reconnect with the peace and comfort there before opening your eyes and coming back to the present.

6. Remember to write down what you have experienced during this exercise and to save these notes for use in part two of this book.

Let Part Two Signify a New Beginning for You

Leaving your spellbound past behind is as easy as turning the pages of this book and moving from part one to part two. As you end "Spellbound in Shadowland," and begin to read "The Awakening," establish the clear intention to be fully present in your life. Refuse to allow yourself to be stuck in the unhappy past for one more precious moment. Acknowledge that you hold the power, right here and right now, to awaken fully to a new state of being. Your new life can be anything you want it to be—inspired by joy and fueled by love. Feel yourself opening to it in this moment, and inviting it in. Your enlightened present awaits your arrival!

Use the chapters that follow as a travel guide for leaving shadowland behind and exploring the light-filled domain that is your true home. Following the path of awakening involves aligning with your Enlightened Spirit, keeping your focus in the present, deactivating your traumatic memories in the now, controlling your thoughts, forgiving yourself and others, and opening to life's blessings.

The fact that you are reading these words indicates that your Spirit is beckoning you, urging you to receive a life of fulfilling experiences, loving relationships, perfect wellness, and abundant blessings. Your Inner Being wants to take your hand and lead you into the glorious realm of magic and wonder where it resides.

Congratulations on hearing and heeding its call for you to embark on a very special journey of personal transformation and enlightenment. Step into the joyous now and feel your Spirit welcoming you home!

PART II:
THE AWAKENING

CHAPTER THREE
REALIGNING WITH THE LIGHT

The phantoms that haunt us cast a fog that prevents us from seeing our inner light. Like ships lost at sea, we wander aimlessly in fear, without a sense of where we are headed, and exhaust ourselves with just managing to stay afloat.

This chapter will assist you in rediscovering the light within you that can guide you safely out of the fog. The beacon that originates from the core of your being will never misdirect you. No doubt there have been times when you have used this inner illumination to navigate life's more difficult straits. Recall an example of when you relied on your inner guidance to deal with a difficult challenge, and the situation turned out even better than you had hoped. Yet, how easy it is to forget the light is there when we are again lost in the murky haze.

Your Enlightened Spirit Is Always There to Help

The radiance that emanates from your center, your Enlightened Spirit, is always there to help in your personal evolution. Only your Inner Being can ultimately assist you in breaking free from your spellbound state. When you align with your Spirit, you allow its light to infuse your body, mind, and emotions. This light eradicates your ghostly phantoms and awakens you to the infinite realm of divine peace, love, and healing. It brings an advanced level of consciousness that reveals untold possibilities for personal and planetary evolution. It enflames your creative potential and stimulates new ideas. Suddenly, you are able to view yourself and your life from a higher perspective—that of your Soul.

As you allow your unique light to shine in the world, you can transform your life so that it is a reflection of your highest and finest Self. Your life becomes a mirror of the truth of who you are, rather than the ghost image you presently see. Since our external world is always the perfect representation of our internal world, our enlightened state ultimately improves our life circumstances. And, although certain changes may be difficult—these are always for the best, and ultimately lead to our greatest joy and satisfaction. We may find that jobs, relationships, and places of living that are not in alignment with our highest good come to an end, either through our own actions or someone else's. Should these endings occur for you, it helps to remember that they are a way of making space in your life for what you truly desire to come to you. We must release the old to make room for the new. It is only that which is not ultimately for your highest good that is likely to change during this enlightenment process.

Access Your Enlightened Spirit by Going Within

So how do you begin to access your Enlightened Spirit? First, by becoming quiet and turning within. In today's fast-paced world, we are usually encouraged to be outer-focused. This means unless we are "doing something productive" many of us are afraid we are wasting time. Too often we compare ourselves to others and determine our personal value on the basis of our accomplishments. We weigh and measure our self worth on the basis of how many books we have read, degrees we have earned, hours we have exercised, opponents we have beaten, pounds we have lost, titles we have attained, or dollars we have accumulated. Compared to these more seductive pursuits, it appears at first that there is little reward for being still and going within. If anything, we feel guilty taking time to feel peaceful in the present when so many things remain on our "to do" list.

What's more, those of us who are haunted would rather do anything than look inside ourselves because we fear what we will find lurking there. If only we can keep ourselves busy enough, there is no danger that we will have a moment free to focus within.

Yet, until we choose to stop everything and turn inside we will never know true peace and fulfillment. In avoiding our inner landscape, we prevent ourselves from accessing our great strength and vast creative potential. What's more, the absence of our attention on the inner realm and that divine spark unwittingly permits our phantoms to gain control over us and our lives.

All of the Answers Are Inside of You

So many of us believe that the answers to our most perplexing problems lie outside of ourselves. We look to friends, family members, teachers, psychic readers, therapists, and even radio talk show hosts to tell us what to do. We allow other people—even those we have never met—to be the ultimate authorities regarding our lives. Yet, in my years of work as a psychotherapist, I have never worked with anyone who did not already have all of their answers within. In fact, I have been awed to discover that everyone—no matter what age, no matter how seemingly lost or confused—ultimately knows the steps to follow to return to the path of integrity, wholeness, and personal fulfillment. While many need help finding the courage to follow that path, deep down, they know exactly in which direction they must go.

The map and accompanying guidebook that reveal the path to your highest good exist in only one place—inside of you. By aligning with the light of your Spirit, you can learn to access and trust those internal resources as your best source of information when you come upon life's crossroads. While it is fine to gain wisdom, support, and encouragement from others, it is important to recognize that the signposts that mark your journey are located on the inner plane.

Your Spirit can only offer assistance when you request it. Ask, and it is always given. You have the world's most gifted counselor, teacher, and mentor right inside of you. Your non-physical counterpart knows you intimately, loves you unconditionally, is always ready and willing to help, and is careful not to intrude. Make it a habit to ask every day for whatever assistance and support you desire. Your answers are always available, sometimes in the form of an inner knowing, other times in the form of the right book or a teacher who comes into your life at the perfect time and place.

By blinding us with fear, our ghosts attempt to prevent us from recognizing the truth that lies within. They tell us that we really can't trust ourselves to know what is right for us, and warn that if we act on our inner guidance, our lives will fall apart. Actually, the reverse is true. That is, until we begin to pay attention to our deeper, spiritual longings, our lives seem to become more and more unsatisfactory. For example, Ardith was a depressed woman working in the same profession she had grown to hate over twenty years. Although she was lonely, bored, and desperately unhappy, she was terrified to make a change. Ardith was attractive, intelligent, creative, hard working, and multi-talented. Yet, whenever she began to dream of returning to school and changing professions, she was paralyzed by fear. Eventually, her life became increasingly intolerable. It was then that Ardith connected with her Inner Being, and found the courage and inspiration to transform her life. She reports that her new job and educational pursuits have brought tremendous joy into her life.

Like Ardith, you can use the support of your Greater Self to identify the path of your highest good and to find the courage to embark upon it. Often this means stepping out of your comfort zone and into new and unexplored territory. And, although this can be frightening, it is ultimately the way of growing into your fullest potential in this lifetime.

Commit to a Daily Mini-Retreat

Daily meditation or visualization is essential for awakening from the spell of the past. A mini-retreat enables you to plug into your true Source, and become recharged; only when you quiet your mind and body, can your Spirit flood your being with its divine light, which uplifts your emotions, promotes healing in your physical body, and brings clarity to your mental state. A daily twenty-minute retreat can provide an antidote to the chaos, stress, and confusion of life. It can help you remain more peaceful, balanced, and centered, regardless of the challenges life sends your way. You can develop greater awareness of what is really important to you, and begin to make choices that are in greater alignment with your fondest desires. You can discover an increased capacity for extending compassion and acceptance to others. And you can fine-tune your ability to access that internal voice of higher wisdom, which is always available if you just become quiet enough to listen. During your daily mini-retreat you may choose to practice more traditional forms of meditation or guided visualizations that employ imagery such as those described in this book.

When and Where to Take Your Mini-Retreat

Select a place for your mini-retreat that is quiet and where you will be undisturbed. Your preferred place might be in a beautiful and tranquil outdoor setting, or it may be in your bedroom or living room. It helps to use the same place each day, so that you begin to associate that location with relaxing and focusing inward. If you are indoors, you may wish to introduce a few items that will enrich your meditative experience and please your senses—like eye pillows, incense or aromatherapy oils, candles, and a compact disc or cassette player with soothing music.

Choose a time when you can relax and focus inward for at least twenty minutes without worrying about being interrupted or feeling so tired that you find it difficult to stay awake. One kindergarten teacher used her thirty-minute morning break for guided imagery. She found a quiet and private spot in the school where she could lie down and listen with her headphones to a guided visualization tape. She used an eye pillow, a flannel sheet, and an aromatherapy spray to make it cozy for herself.

Meditation Is a Natural Process

Meditation provides practice in stopping the mind's incessant chatter, and connecting with our true Essence—which is always there, but often is drowned out by the noise of our thoughts. Many believe that meditation is difficult, and that years of special instruction are required to meditate properly. Nothing could be further from the truth. Meditation is the most natural experience in the world. It is you connecting with your Deeper Self, in the quiet and calm of your being. It is your opportunity to enter the sacred space within, and to bask in the love and peace that awaits you there. It is as simple as closing your eyes and focusing on your breathing, or the silent space between each breath.

Choose anything you would like to focus on. It may be the rise and fall of your chest as you breathe, the flame of a candle, the song of a bird, the sound of a fountain, or a word or phrase which is silently repeated and synchronized with your breathing. Some individuals prefer to count from one to five and back, while others select a particular word or phrase that means something to them, such as "I am love," "peace," or a favorite line from a prayer. While concentrating on the point of focus, you will notice that your mind will naturally wander to your "to do" list or to thoughts and feelings associated with past or future events. The task is to gently redirect the attention back to whatever you are choosing to focus on, without judging yourself or becoming frustrated. Think of how you would take the hand of a toddler who has noticed something shiny in the next aisle of a department store and started to wander toward it. Your mind is like that small child, needing frequent guidance to get it back on track.

In his profound book, *The Power of Now,* Eckhart Tolle suggests focusing on our invisible, inner body as a form of meditation. This is a wonderful way of transcending the mind and experiencing the presence of your Spirit. Just close your eyes, go into the silent space within, and focus on the life force in your hands, your feet, your arms, and your legs. Next, feel the invisible network of energy that breathes movement and sensation into every cell; sense the entire pattern of energy that forms your invisible inner body as a complete, dynamic, whole. Try not to get too attached to what it might look like. Rather, just feel it. This experience of mindless attention takes you into the place beyond the mind where your Spirit resides—that place of Oneness with the Divine.

This is not to say you will always experience peace as you meditate. In fact, more often than not those who meditate report that they are not doing it right, because their mind continues to wander and distract them from the point of focus. But this is a misconception. Whenever you are engaged in the process of meditation, even if your mind wanders one hundred times during your twenty-minute session, you are doing it right. The goal is just to do it—not to accomplish any particular state of mind, body or spirit. Research shows that those who meditate regularly experience many rewards that extend far beyond the meditation session itself. Better physical health, greater peace of mind, and a clearer connection with the spiritual realm are among the many benefits.

Meditation allows you to witness your mind's activities with detachment. Just the process of observing our thoughts and refocusing our attention when our mind wanders helps to foster inner peace and teaches us that we are more than our minds. As Fritz Perls, the famous Gestalt therapist, used to say, "Lose your mind and come to your senses." Although our minds have great value, as long as we identify with them, we are in for an emotional roller coaster ride. It is only when we learn to be the observer of our own thoughts that we can discover the deep sense of calm and well-being that exists beyond our mind's endless chatter. What's more, we can learn to control our minds in our everyday lives, rather than allowing them to control us.

Exercise #4
The Universe Within Meditation

1. Take a moment to sit in meditation. Find a comfortable place to sit, either on a straight-backed chair or on the ground with your legs folded. Make sure it is quiet and that you will not be interrupted for 15 to 20 minutes.

2. Imagine that a beautiful beam of light is coming down from the heavens, directly into the top of

your head. Feel this uplifting, radiant light filling your entire being. Take your awareness into your body, focus on the atoms, and the vast spaces between the atoms that are absorbing this light. These spaces are proportionately as vast as the spaces between stars in the heavens. Focus on the magnificent universe that exists within you. Go into these silent spaces with your awareness, and observe.

3. If your mind begins to wander, or chatter about this and that, just observe it without judgment and gently take your attention back into the universe within you. Go again into the silent, vast, spaces between the atoms, and just allow yourself to be. There is nothing to do, accomplish, see, or learn. At some point, you will find yourself feeling very peaceful, and in a state of mindless awareness. Again, just notice.

4. When you are ready to return, do so slowly, and gradually. Open your eyes, and come back to this time and place. Congratulate yourself on having taken the time to visit the sacred space within, no matter what the experience was like for you. The practice itself is what matters most—not the outcome.

5. Make some notes about what you experienced during this meditation.

Guided Visualizations Are a Tool for Establishing Contact

Guided visualizations such as those you have experienced in part one are another excellent tool for establishing contact with your Spirit. You may wish to use cassette tapes or compact discs to lead you through relaxation and imagery exercises while soothing music plays in the background. Visit bookstores and research the Internet for such tapes. There are also guided visualizations on compact disc to accompany this book.

The following process provides an opportunity to meet your Enlightened Spirit and begin to access your inner radiance. As mentioned previously, it is important that you allow yourself to *play with your imagination* during this process, holding a lighthearted, curious attitude. Trying too hard, or approaching this with too much heaviness or seriousness can defeat the purpose. If you have trouble imagining or experiencing something suggested here, simply *pretend* that you are seeing, feeling, or hearing something.

Exercise #5
The Beacon

1. Put your body in a comfortable position, close your eyes, and take several long, slow, deep breaths. Feel yourself breathing in peace, up through the soles of your feet, and breathing out tension and stress.

2. Imagine yourself again in your heart sanctuary. Sense the beauty, tranquility, and safety, and notice how good it feels to be here. Become reacquainted with all of its familiar sights, sensations, sounds, and smells. Feel each of your cells becoming satu-

rated with the peaceful, gentle, nurturing light of your heart sanctuary, as you surrender to the serenity and comfort of this sacred space.

3. Pretend there is a figure approaching who is your Enlightened Spirit. It may appear to be a person, or just a bright light. Observe everything you can about this beautiful being, as you bask in its radiant presence. Feel yourself opening up to receive the love it is sending you. Think of how you feel about someone you adore, perhaps a child or a special animal, and then picture your Non-Physical Self feeling that same way about you. Allow the love to wash over you like a warm wave that penetrates to the center of your being. Imagine there is a deep well within you and the love of your Spirit is filling this well to the brim.

4. Take this opportunity to ask your Inner Being for any guidance or assistance you would like. You may receive an answer immediately, or it may come sometime during the next few weeks. Just be open to whatever form the answer may take, and know it will come at the right time and place and in the perfect way.

5. Next, your Spirit gives you a gift in the form of a special beacon. Take a moment to examine your beacon, noticing how it looks and feels. You will observe that as you shine your beacon on any aspect of your life, you are able to view that situa-

tion with greater clarity and a higher perspective. Your beacon's light penetrates to the core of whatever it touches, and dissolves anything that obscures your deepest truth. With your beacon, you are able to obtain a greater level of understanding and make decisions that are in alignment with your highest good. You can also use your beacon in future visualizations to see clearly into the shadows of your consciousness and to expose your ghosts to the light of your Spiritual Essence.

6. Take a moment now to direct your beacon toward an area of your life in which you would like more spiritual light, and just observe what happens. Notice any changes that take place in the scene, or any insights that occur to you. Again, you may find that the effects of shining your beacon on this situation become increasingly apparent to you in the coming weeks.

7. Find a safe place in which to store your beacon, so you can retrieve it easily in the future. Feel free to linger in your heart sanctuary for as long as you like. When you are ready, return slowly and gradually back to the room and this time and space, bringing the peaceful feelings back with you.

Take a moment to record on paper your experiences during this exercise. What surprised you most about that visualization? What insights or observations did you bring back with you?

Practice this visualization on a regular basis as a means of establishing a clear and strong connection to your Inner Being.

Being Mindful

Our ghosts prefer that we waste our precious lives either focusing on our unhappy past or worrying about what is yet to come. In our phantom-induced spell we are oblivious to the most important time of all, and the only time there is: the present moment. Whenever you choose to focus on the Now, you make it impossible for the ghosts to impact you. The ghosts prefer to have you agonizing about what did or didn't happen, or fearing what might or might not happen. These activities keep you disconnected from the point of power within you, which is only accessible in the present. It is in *this* moment that you hold the power to create the life you desire. It is in *this* moment that you are capable of smelling a rose, biting into a juicy apple, or smiling at your beloved.

If you allow them to, the ghosts will keep you distracted from the one time that matters most of all. They will seduce you with catastrophic thoughts of what could go wrong in the future, and hypnotize you with a litany of your past mistakes, allowing each precious moment to slip by, beyond your awareness.

Any time you become mindful of the present moment, you awaken from your ghost-induced trance. As you allow your senses to drink in the experience of the now, you may be surprised to discover that in *this moment*, all is well. Chances are you are safe and have what you truly need in this moment. And within this instant lies an infinite array of creative possibilities.

As you discover the potential for joy that exists in each moment of your existence, you begin to dance to your life's own music, and to discover that the power for writing your song and choreographing your steps exists right now. It is not the song you played years ago that is important. Rather, it is the note and the step you choose right now, and from this moment forward, which matter most.

Many of us play the same depressing melody year after year, because we are accustomed to it. Until we are conscious in the present, we are oblivious to the power we hold to compose a song that makes our heart sing and our body feel electric with life force energy.

Learning how to be mindful in the present is a challenge; the following exercise is designed to help you practice focusing your awareness in the now.

Exercise #6
Practicing Mindfulness

For this process you will need at least twenty minutes alone in a natural setting. Begin by walking during the first part of this exercise. Your goal is to remain aware of what you experience through all of your senses during the entire time. In order to keep yourself focused on what you perceive in the moment, from time to time finish each of the following sentences.

"Right now I am seeing _____."
"Right now I am hearing _____."
"Right now I am feeling _____."
"Right now I am smelling _____."
"Right now I am tasting _____."

Attempt to notice everything you can about your surroundings. Pretend that you are seeing, hearing, feeling, tasting, and smelling things for the first time, and try to notice new things about these sensations. Next, sit down for a few minutes and close your eyes in order to focus more on what you hear, feel, and smell.

Should you find that your mind has wandered away from the present, simply bring your awareness back to what you perceive in the moment.

Afterwards, record in your journal some of your experiences and observations.

Do this exercise as often as you can; practice being present in your life.

Make it your daily intent to catch yourself when you have left the now and bring yourself back to it. Each time you go through this process, you disempower your inner phantoms and further align with your Spirit. It is impossible for you to be under the spell of your past when you are mindful in the present.

A good way to know when you have left the now is to notice how you are feeling. Generally, if you are feeling bad: worried, anxious, guilty, resentful, or fearful, your negative mind has again led you astray. Once you recognize this, it is only a matter of returning to the only time there is—the present moment.

Other Ways to Replenish Your Spiritual Resources

In addition to taking daily mini-retreats, and being mindful, it is important to engage in everyday activities that replenish you spiritually. Here are some options.

Keep a Journal

Journal writing is a way of maintaining a conversation with the many diverse parts of you. Through journaling, you can strengthen your connection to your spiritual center, and learn more about your desires, emotions, beliefs, and life purpose. You can become more consciously aware of inner conflicts and explore ways of resolving them. You can record your goals and entertain creative ways of attaining them.

Spend Time in Nature

Visiting a beach, desert, forest, mountain, or meadow can help you to feel more connected to the Earth and to your Deepest Self. The natural world speaks to our Spiritual Essence, if we simply listen to it. In the solitude of a forest or desert, we can more easily tune in and hear the whispers of our Inner Being.

Plant a Garden

Sometimes a connection to the sacred may be found in our own yard. Tending a flower or vegetable garden can help you become attuned with the earth's rhythms and appreciate the beauty, perfection, and diversity of all of life. Working in the soil grounds us and connects us to the centuries of humans who preceded us in cultivating the earth. As we watch nature's abundance unfold, we are reminded of the fertile soil of consciousness, within which we may plant and sprout new seeds of creative potential.

Interact with Animals

Our companion animals can open our hearts as they offer their precious gift of unconditional love. Even the most emotionally defended person can find it safe to love a cat or a dog deeply and completely. Animals receive us as we are, without judgment. They teach us about forgiveness and about living in the present moment. Through animals we can experience our kinship to all of nature and recognize that all life is truly sacred.

Read Uplifting Books

Visit a bookstore or library, and see which books call out to you from their shelves; books that touch your Spiritual Core will help you feel uplifted and experience greater enlightenment. Keep some favorites next to your bed to read just before you go to sleep or when you first awaken. And whenever you are feeling fearful, let these texts broaden your perspective and remind you of higher truths.

Listen to Beautiful Music

There are so many gifted artists creating music that can transport us to profound inner spaces. Many stores now have listening stations so you can hear compact discs before purchasing them. Find music you love, and then make the time to relax, close your eyes, and let the music transport you on an inward journey. I have listed some of my favorites at the end of this book.

Get Physical

Besides giving you added energy and lifting your mood, exercise can shift your focus to the present moment and provide a wonderful "brain break." Some find that walking, jogging, swimming, biking, dancing, rowing or roller-blading gives them a kind of spiritual "high." Others are attracted to the inner glow they experience in the aftermath of a Yoga, Pilates, or Tai Chi session. What's important is that you find some physical activities you enjoy and do them regularly.

Follow Your Dreams

Your dreams are a symbolic source of communication from your deeper self; dreams almost always reveal things to us about ourselves that we weren't consciously aware of. Your dreams will help you find your true path, and let you know when you have deviated from it. They will show you where you are "hung-up" on old patterns of behavior, and even offer solutions for getting unstuck. Keep a notebook or a tape recorder near your bed so you can maintain a record of your dreams; as you pay more attention to them, you are more likely to remember your dreams. There are also books, teachers, and dream groups to help you discover the messages your Dream Self is delivering to you.

Worship

Attending services at a church, synagogue, or temple can be another way of recharging your spiritual batteries. Many people find that their religious affiliations provide opportunities to connect with like-minded souls and to experience a sense of spiritual community. Religious rituals can act as a doorway to sacred territory, helping us to honor the presence of the Divine in our lives.

Form a Support Network

It helps to have a group of friends and/or family who have made their own spiritual growth a priority and who are able to share insights and encouragement with you. Surround yourself with people who are loving, kind, and respectful of you. Your support network can assist you in seeing through the illusions cast by the ghosts who attempt to manipulate you with fear. Seek others who share your path, so you can help each other find the way from darkness into light.

Create Something

When you access your creativity, you tap into the life force that flows through the core of your being, whether you are writing, painting, crocheting, sculpting, quilting, building, beading, carving, or cooking. If you have difficulty accessing the artist within you, *The Artist's Way* by Julia Cameron and Mark Bryan is a wonderful book that includes exercises to help you align yourself with the creative energy of the universe. It is the *process* of creative self-expression, rather than what you produce, that offers great personal rewards. Discover your multidimensional nature as you give yourself permission to play creatively.

Practice Gratitude

Whenever we focus on what we are grateful for, we add more light to our lives. It is so easy to focus on what is missing in our lives, or what is less than perfect. We are bombarded with images in the media of what we should want to have in order to be happy—the right car, the right partner, the right clothes. But simply by redirecting our attention toward what we already have, we can lift our Spirits and maintain a healthier perspective. We can recognize all of the things that we may be taking for granted: good health, loving friends and family, sunshine, abundant water, nourishing food, fulfilling work—life itself!

Whenever you feel down, try to finish the sentence, "I am grateful for..." as many times as you can. Over and over again, list out loud the many things for which you are grateful. Within minutes, you will feel lighter and more positive about the day.

Oprah recommends that each of us list five things we are grateful for at the end of each day. This is certainly a wonderful way to count your blessings. However you choose to do it, make sure you take time to appreciate what is right in your life every day.

Give Generously

It is often said that you get what you give. Giving of yourself—whether your time and energy, your money or all three—reconnects you with your Spirit. Experience the joy and fulfillment that come with doing something special to help someone less fortunate. Nothing feels better than to know you have made someone's day a little brighter. Offer your support to those organizations whose mission is to make the world a better place in ways that matter to you. Add your voice to the chorus of those who are speaking for those who cannot speak for themselves.

Even your good thoughts and prayers for others matter—more than you may know. Larry Dossey is a physician who summarized research on the effectiveness of prayer in his book, *Healing Words*. He has found considerable evidence that prayer works, and that general prayers for the best possible outcome (without specifying what that might be) seem to be the most effective, although prayers for specific outcomes also produce results. It doesn't seem to matter if the person doing the praying knows the one being prayed for, or if the recipient of the prayers is near or far away. Experiments reveal that a wide array of physical ailments have been positively affected by prayer—from heart attacks and headaches, to wounds, tumors, and high blood pressure. Both animals and plants responded favorably to prayer as well.

Make it a habit to send good thoughts to others, both known and unknown to you, during the day. And be on the lookout for opportunities to practice random acts of kindness whenever possible. Every act of giving does make a difference, no matter how seemingly small or insignificant. When you practice generosity, you become a guidepost directing humanity toward its brightest possible future.

Exercise #7
Committing to a Spiritual Practice

1. If you are not already doing so, are you willing to commit to taking a mini-retreat of at least twenty minutes each day? If so, when and where will you take this mini-retreat? How will you spend the time? When do you plan to begin? What do you need to do to make sure you honor this commitment to yourself?

2. List the things you are already doing that replenish your spiritual resources.

3. What old and new activities would you be willing to commit to doing on a regular basis to replenish your spiritual resources? How, when, and where do you plan to make this happen for yourself?

4. Follow through on your plan.

Following the Path of Spiritual Growth

As you cultivate certain qualities such as inner peace, acceptance, personal responsibility, integrity, and joyfulness, you break the spell of your past and step into the glorious now. Your spiritual evolution is your personal fortification against the destructive impact of the ghosts that haunt you. Like Dorothy and her companions who were safe as long as they remained on the yellow brick road, the phantoms cannot besiege you when you are following your spiritual path. Let us examine some of the guideposts you can use to stay on course and avoid being lured off track.

Choosing Peace

Inner peace is an antidote to the fear that the ghosts wield as their most powerful weapon; since fear and peace cannot coexist, every moment you choose to be peaceful is a moment in which you are free of the phantom's grasp. The ghosts cannot touch you when you are bathed in the peace of your Spirit.

When you are feeling tranquil, you are most attuned to your inner wisdom. It is from a place of deep calm that you can hear the whispers of your Soul and find your deepest truth. Like a radio adjusted to eliminate the static, serenity brings clarity to the broadcast of your inner guidance.

A peaceful state is healthy for your body. During periods of rest and inner calm, you press the off button on the body's stress reaction; your body relishes deep relaxation as a way of revitalizing itself. When you maintain a state of calm, you give your cells an opportunity to restore themselves to optimal levels of functioning; while stress ultimately weakens your immune system, a peaceful state provides the ideal conditions for its strengthening and rejuvenation.

Many of us spend our lives in a state of constant turmoil, waiting for situations outside ourselves to change so that we can finally feel peace. The problem with this approach is that there will always be situations around us that will stress us if we allow them to. Our power lies not in controlling the situations, people, or events in our lives, but in controlling our *reactions* to them.

Though it is a challenge to remain at peace in the midst of a busy and demanding life, you can learn to spend increasing amounts of time feeling calm and serene. One way of experiencing more tranquility is to engage in your daily spiritual practice. In addition, it helps to have a gentle way of reminding yourself to relax when you catch yourself becoming uptight. The following exercise is designed with that purpose in mind.

Exercise #8
Choosing Peace

Whenever you notice yourself feeling anxious, fearful, or upset, take a few slow, deep breaths and say to yourself: **"I choose peace instead of this."**

A good way to make sure you are breathing deeply is to begin by forcefully exhaling completely. The next inhalation will be a deep breath. It will feel as if your abdomen (below your navel) is a balloon being filled with air. As you exhale, you will notice your abdomen flattening.

With practice, you can train yourself to remember to choose peace when you would normally feel distress. Make an agreement with yourself to use certain signals throughout the day as a reminder to take some deep breaths and choose peace. For example, you can decide to take a deep breath and say "I choose peace instead of this" every time you hear the phone ring, or before making a call.

Practice when you are driving in heavy traffic, or late for an appointment. Remind yourself to breathe deeply and choose peace when your children are squabbling, or when you are opening your bills. Let each of life's little challenges be an opportunity to demonstrate your commitment to inviting greater serenity into your life.

Practicing Acceptance

When you accept what life brings to you, you align with your Spirit. Acceptance doesn't mean you are passive when faced with an unpleasant circumstance. Rather, it means you don't waste emotional energy feeling sorry for yourself, blaming yourself or others, or resenting the situation in which you find yourself. Acceptance is making peace with your present conditions—no matter how difficult they may be, or unfair they seem; it is holding the premise that everything ultimately happens for your highest good, as you view the big picture of your life through the eyes of your Inner Being. Acceptance takes you to a place of inner strength and clarity, which can serve you well during life's challenging moments.

Practice acceptance in little ways, when you experience life's inevitable little disappointments; each day provides us with countless opportunities to accept that which is beyond our control. This will help you to move to a place of inner balance and calm more quickly should you be confronted with a major crisis. Once you have ceased resisting what life brings you each moment, you will be in a much better position to decide what action, if any, needs to be taken, and then to follow through on your chosen course.

Developing Personal Responsibility

When we accept personal responsibility, we focus our energy and attention on what we can do to heal our selves and improve our lives. Rather than pointing the finger at others, as our ghosts would have us do, we take a good, long, honest look in the mirror and ask what we are doing to contribute to our suffering, and what we need to do to make things better. We address our deficiencies and build upon our strengths. We recognize that we have choices and hold ourselves accountable for our actions.

Holding ourselves accountable does not mean we are hard on ourselves and fail to forgive ourselves for our shortcomings; nor does it mean that we live in the past and berate ourselves repeatedly for our failures. It is best to be gentle with yourself, to let go of the past, while also acknowledging mistakes and learning from them.

Our society does not encourage us to take responsibility for ourselves. When something bad happens, we often seek someone to blame. Rarely are we advised to ask ourselves, "What did I do to contribute to this negative situation?" There appear to be great financial rewards for pinning the blame on others in our litigious society.

Yet, I question where such thinking places us on the path to spiritual enlightenment. I believe that a truly evolved person is one who has learned to be accountable for his or her actions, and to forgive both self and others. When we assume personal responsibility we demonstrate our intention to profit from life's challenges by strengthening our character, becoming more humble, and addressing our shortcomings.

Beware of Victimhood

Sadly, some individuals prefer to use their wounds from the past to excuse themselves and to control or manipulate others. Carolyn Myss (author of *Anatomy of the Spirit* and *Why People Don't Heal*

And How They Can) tells us that individuals who engage in "woundology" may demand special treatment from others because they are "broken." They may expect others to feel sorry for them, not hold them accountable, or accept their bad behavior, because after all, they were traumatized in their childhood. Their needs are supposed to be more important than the needs of others because they are wounded.

These individuals are stuck in a victim mentality, and use every opportunity to blame others for their unhappiness. Rather than looking at what they could be doing to help themselves, they remain miserable and claim it is everyone else's fault. They may use their unhealed injuries as an excuse for not moving forward in life: "How can you expect me to finish college, when I was abused as a child?" "I'm too wounded to get a real job." "Of course I can't have an intimate relationship with another person, I was sexually abused as a child."

There is no question that traumatic episodes in our childhood impact us greatly, as early chapters of this book have emphasized. However, the person who engages in woundology does not aim to heal the wounds of the past and become whole again. Instead, this individual wears his or her suffering like a badge that says, "Take pity on me."

Have Faith in Yourself

Our phantoms are good at instilling feelings of hopelessness in us. "I will never get better. Things will never change. I can't change." But in spite of what our inner tormentors tell us, we can heal from any tragedy, no matter how awful. You are so much more powerful and amazing than you think you are. You are a vast, creative, multi-dimensional being with unlimited potential. Believe in your ability to get through your current difficulties. Know that your Spirit is beautiful and resilient.

Ruth is a lovely woman in her sixties who worked with me in therapy to heal the emotional wounds from abuse she suffered in childhood. When it was time for us to terminate our work together, she had a dream in which she entered a small building known to house a child who had experienced "terrible injuries that broke her into pieces." Her fear was that there would be nothing left of the child. To Ruth's amazement, as she stepped into a darkened room, she saw a pedestal with a bell jar on top of it, filled with a beautiful liquid-like substance that she knew to be the child's soul. Upon seeing the Spirit of the child, she fell to her knees and whispered "I see you," gazing in reverence and awe at the most beautiful, perfect, pure, clear, radiant light she had ever seen. As the child's Spirit glowed in a multitude of colors that illuminated the room, Ruth knew that she was in the presence of something very sacred.

Ruth's dream reassured her that none of the abuse she had endured had harmed the beauty and perfection of her Spirit. Like Ruth, you have the capacity to heal yourself and your life, for nothing you have endured in life has marred the essence of who you are—a magnificent being of light having a physical experience in this time and place.

Demonstrate Integrity

When you demonstrate integrity, you align yourself with the highest and the best within you. Your integrity is your personal honor code; it is your willingness to make difficult and sometimes unpopular choices based on your own ethics and principles. It is not rigid adherence to external rules and voices of authority, it is living in accordance with your internal sense of what is right for you.

A university student I once had the pleasure of teaching told our class a heart-breaking story about when she was in the seventh grade in a public school in Florida in the 1950's. On one memorable day, a new girl, an African-American, came to the school. The teacher ordered all of the students to line up and spit in the little girl's chair before the new pupil was allowed to sit down. My student was the only one who refused to spit in the chair, and she was suspended from school for disobeying the teacher's order.

It takes courage to act with integrity. Sometimes, like my student, we suffer short-term negative consequences for choosing the high road. But these are never as great as the long-term consequences we experience when we sell our souls for approval, acceptance, fame, or fortune.

Living with integrity means your thoughts, words, and deeds are congruent with what you believe and what you value. It means telling the truth to others, and also to your self. Many people lie to themselves in order to justify behavior they know violates their personal moral code. "I know I shouldn't be cruel, but he deserved it." "I am over-charging for this service or merchandise, but this customer can afford it." "I'm not going to tell the clerk that she short-changed herself because this chain store has plenty of money." "I can call in sick even though I'm fine because I have earned a day off." How many of us are experts at rationalizing our choices to our selves and others? How often do we look the other way as we violate our own sense of fairness and justice?

When you stray from the path of integrity, you make yourself more vulnerable to the destructive influence of the ghosts that haunt you. Conversely, following your inner truth and wisdom will keep you aligned with your Inner Being and on the path of personal growth and fulfillment.

The first step in the process of choosing integrity is to take a good, long, and completely honest look in the mirror *without judging what you see reflected there*. None of us is perfect, and the willingness to openly appraise your motives is a huge step in the right direction. Rather than criticizing what you see, focus on the way in which you intend to grow. Accept that you are human, and make a commitment to pay more heed to your personal ethics from this day forward. One thing is certain, life will continue to provide you with many opportunities to practice exercising your integrity muscle!

The next exercise is an opportunity to access your deepest personal truth regarding a difficult situation.

Exercise #9
Choosing Integrity

1. Think of an area of your life in which you are faced with a difficult decision. List all the options you can think of for dealing with this situation.

2. Close your eyes, take a few deep breaths, return to your heart sanctuary, and ask yourself what you are to learn in this situation, as you shine your beacon on it. Every crisis or challenge placed in front of us offers an opportunity for personal growth. For example, is this about being more loving and compassionate, being kind, being honest, being responsible, being humble, being patient, being courageous, standing up for yourself, honoring your

commitments, demonstrating reverence for life, demonstrating self-respect, or speaking your truth while respecting others?

3. One at a time, picture yourself taking each of the actions you listed in step one for dealing with this situation. With your eyes closed, ask yourself how each potential action would or would not foster the areas of personal growth you have identified in step two. Imagine how you would feel about yourself should you take each of the actions you have listed.

4. Open your eyes, and write about what you have learned. You may already know what action you wish to take in this situation, or you may need more time to ponder your various options.

Lightening Up

Anytime you are feeling joyful, lighthearted, or enthusiastic, you are in tune with your Spiritual Essence. When you lighten up, you open up to allow more of the light within to shine outward; that inner radiance is like a beam that illuminates the pathway to even more joyful life experiences. Follow your bliss, and it will lead you to the fulfillment of your higher purpose.

Your phantoms will tell you to wait until your life is perfect to be happy. They are always willing to point out the things that are wrong with your present circumstances, and caution you that the only way to solve your problems is to approach them with grave seriousness. Yet, the only effect of dwelling in negative emotions is that nothing is likely to change for the better.

Happiness can be found, moment-by-moment, if you look for it. Make it your objective to find a reason to lighten up, and notice that the longer you hold good feelings, the more reasons you can find to feel even better. Decide that you are going to enjoy each day to the fullest, and then let life surprise you with new and delightful ways of finding and receiving pleasure.

CHAPTER FOUR
RESTORING EMOTIONAL VITALITY

One of the most effective ways of awakening from your spellbound state is to **briefly** revisit those traumas in which the ghosts first shrouded you in darkness, to shine the light of present awareness upon them. When you return to the scenes in which the phantoms established their territory in the shadows of your consciousness, you are able to neutralize the spell they have cast upon you. Exercises two and three in chapter two were meant to help you identify the traumatic scenes that are currently holding you hostage. This chapter provides an overview for how to work with those scenes in order to break free from the past, and awaken to your joyous now.

The purpose of briefly recalling painful events of your past is not to re-experience the original traumas, but rather to bring them into the luminous present. You do this by using your imagination to **rewrite** those scenes in a way that reduces or dispels their negative impact on your life. A rewritten scene is not meant to replace the original memory, but rather to heal its harmful effects.

In order to prepare yourself for this approach, the following exercise is an opportunity for you to evoke a happy memory from your childhood to give your current adult self and your inner child an opportunity to meet in a positive setting.

Exercise #10
Meeting Your Inner Child

1. Make yourself comfortable, close your eyes, and begin taking long, slow, relaxing breaths. Imagine that you are again amidst the beauty, safety, and peace of your heart sanctuary. Take a moment to reacquaint yourself with this tranquil setting in all its detail. Notice the sights, sounds, smells, and sensations present there.

2. Picture yourself surrounded in your heart sanctuary with a magnificent bubble of light. Pretend that the bubble begins to float you back in time, back to a happy scene from your childhood. Just allow the bubble to transport you to a joyful time when you were still a child.

3. Once you have arrived at the pleasant childhood event, notice everything you can about your younger self, and what is happening in the scene. Pay particular attention to how your younger self is feeling. If you can't remember a happy time, simply imagine one as you wish it had been.

4. Then imagine that your present self is stepping into the scene. Perhaps the child sees a friendly stranger approaching. When you get close enough, introduce yourself to your younger self. Tell the child "I am you, all grown up. I've come to get to know you."

5. Spend some time interacting with the child. Learn all you can about him or her. Imagine that you play together. If you and the child feel comfortable, pretend you hold the child on your lap. Tell the child you love him or her, and that he or she is precious to you.

6. When you are ready, you may wish to make the scene of the adult and the child very little, and put it in your heart surrounded by love. Then come back to the present, feeling clear-headed and alert.

Guidelines for Rewriting Traumas

Your imagination is one of your most powerful tools for awakening from your spellbound state. When you revisit a traumatic episode in your mind's eye, you have the opportunity to set things right. You can create the scene just the way you would have liked for it to have been. You can finish your unfinished business, and resolve the unresolved. You can say the things you would have liked to have said, and do the things you would have liked to have done. In facing your shadowy intruders, you transform them so that they no longer have power over you. The only requirement is a willingness to engage your imagination.

It is important to pretend that your current, adult self is present with your younger self in the scene you are recreating. This enables you to access the light, wisdom, courage, strength, and greater awareness of your present self as you come face-to-face with your phantoms. Through your adult self, you are able to shine the light of conscious awareness on the memory and awaken from the spell it had cast upon you.

Often people are surprised at what they discover when they revisit their traumas and view them through adult lenses. For example, one forty-five year old woman was haunted by the memory of a rape that occurred almost twenty-five years before. She was afraid to leave the house, for fear of encountering the rapist. When she used her imagination to envision her present, adult self at the scene of the rape, she was surprised to discover that her attacker was "just a boy." From the perspective of her forty-five-year old self, he no longer seemed threatening to her.

It is often best to work with a trained psychotherapist when rewriting traumatic events, for several reasons. First, having someone witness your process makes the experience more valid and consequently, heightens its effectiveness. Second, it can be frightening to confront your ghosts, and it is often comforting to have a safe person accompany you to those dark places within. Third, a therapist can guide you through the process, so that you can focus more completely on what you are experiencing in the moment. And fourth, the therapist can ensure that you banish your ghosts and awaken from your spellbound state without being re-traumatized.

When we revisit a distressing event from our past with our adult self, exactly what might we rewrite? To answer this question, let's return to the chart on the components of spellbound behavior as it was presented in chapter one.

During the Initial Trauma a Person Will:	In the Present Situation the One Who Is Spellbound Will:
1. Feel strong emotions	1. Re-experience the same emotions
2. Feel like a powerless victim	2. Feel like a powerless victim
3. Make limiting decisions	3. Reinforce those limiting decisions
4. Lose parts of the self	4. Remain disconnected from parts of the self
5. Become fixated at the age when the initial trauma occurred	5. Feel and behave as if at the age when the initial trauma occurred

When we rewrite a past scene that is haunting us, it is best to deal with each of the five components listed above. This is summarized in the following chart:

During the Initial Trauma a Person Will:	In Rewriting the Traumatic Scene a Person Can:
1. Feel strong emotions	1. Release unexpressed emotions
2. Feel like a powerless victim	2. Restore a sense of personal power
3. Make limiting decisions	3. Revise limiting decisions
4. Lose parts of the self	4. Reclaim lost parts of the self
5. Become fixated at the age when the initial trauma occurred	5. Rekindle the development of fixated parts

Each of the components that may be involved in rewriting a traumatic event is discussed briefly below.

1. Releasing Unexpressed Emotions

As long as a traumatic event generates an emotional charge, you remain under the ghosts' spell. By neutralizing the emotions associated with a past scene, you can awaken from the trance that holds you captive. Thus, in rewriting traumatic episodes, it is essential that you involve both your mind and your emotions. Going through the process from the neck up is not going to have the same impact as allowing your self to feel all of the feelings associated with the targeted event.

It is often frightening to even consider revisiting the emotions associated with a painful memory. Often we have spent years successfully avoiding contact with those feelings. We may fear that once we open the door to the pain we hold within, we will drown in it. We may believe that we will fall apart emotionally if we allow ourselves to access the overpowering rage, grief, shame, or hurt that is associated with the trauma.

Such fears allow the ghosts to maintain their spell. It is by both *feeling* and then *releasing* the emotions you have stockpiled that you free yourself from spellbound behavior. Some people are able to feel the emotions, but hold on to them for various reasons. This simply prolongs and intensifies the spell that the trauma has cast upon them. Others believe they have released their emotions, but have only avoided them by pushing them deeper into the shadows of their consciousness. Again, this only perpetuates the trance.

There is another important reason for letting go of the negative emotions we store within. These warehoused feelings affect our body chemistry and they can literally make us sick over time.

Hold on to enough bitter resentment and you just might end up with an ulcer. In contrast, happiness and peace-of-mind seem to be the optimal state for maintaining our physical and mental health. When we release our emotional baggage, we create the space for greater serenity and increased joy in our lives.

To access the feelings associated with a trauma, it isn't necessary to re-live the event. I have found that if people take themselves back in their mind's eye to a few minutes before the trauma actually occurred, they are usually able to feel the emotions that are connected to the scene without having to re-experience the actual episode.

The emotions we most likely stockpile—anger, hurt, guilt, and shame—are each discussed below.

We may hold resentment, bitterness, or rage toward someone we believe wronged us. But regardless of what that person may have done to us, it is only ourselves we are hurting by storing angry feelings within. What's more, until we release the anger from our past, it is likely to emerge at inappropriate times and places. And, we never know what may trigger one of our embarrassing explosions.

Often there is tremendous grief, sadness, and pain associated with our most traumatic memories. We may store this hurt for decades, like an infected boil that festers within. As we attempt to safeguard that boil from being touched, we put more and more energy into self-protection and less and less into constructive endeavors. Although it hurts to lance the boil so that it may heal, it cannot compare with the agony and personal expense of living with the boil for years on end.

I have observed that most of us are able to feel either hurt or anger regarding our traumatic past, but have difficulty accessing both of these emotions. Some people can cry and readily express their sadness, but they have trouble feeling any anger. Others express outrage over an event, but are unable to access the pain associated with the experience. Generally, I have found that the greatest healing takes place when we are able to feel and release the emotion that is most difficult for us to "own."

It is common for us to blame ourselves for the traumatic events we have endured—even when it is totally illogical to do so. We may believe that our parents divorced because we were bad, or that we deserved to be beaten by an abusive parent. We may tell ourselves, "If only I hadn't done X, then this terrible thing wouldn't have happened." Even when we made choices that did ultimately hurt us, it does absolutely no good to continue feeling guilty. Certainly, we benefit from learning from our mistakes. But once we have figured out the lesson from our experience, it is essential that we forgive ourselves and move on. Too often we use guilt to needlessly punish ourselves. You must be willing to release your feelings of guilt from the past in order to be healthy in the present.

Often there are feelings of humiliation, dishonor, and embarrassment associated with our traumatic past, which erode self-respect and self-worth. This toxic shame casts a dark shadow on our efforts and accomplishments. It colors everything we do as not good enough, and everything we are as devoid of value. It marks us as human garbage, undeserving of love or happiness. Shame is experienced below the neck. Many abuse survivors report that they know in their heads they are worthwhile, but in their hearts they feel worthless.

Ultimately, the goal of rewriting a scene is to deactivate its emotional charge. How do you know when you have accomplished this objective? When you are able to recall a traumatic event with emotional detachment. The charge has been neutralized when you can think about what happened without feeling an emotional tug. This does not mean you have forgotten what happened to you. It means you no longer allow that event to control you in the present.

2. Feel Powerful and Right the Wrongs

In rewriting traumatic episodes, we give ourselves the opportunity to feel victorious rather than victimized. We reclaim our power and use it to right any wrongs that may have been done to us or that we may have done to others. We confront our fears and take charge of our lives. Instead of experiencing helplessness, we can discover what it is like to feel and be our most capable selves.

With the assistance of your current (adult) self in the safety of your imagination, you can ward off an attacker, stand up for yourself with a bully, or rescue yourself from a dangerous situation. You can say the words you were afraid to say, and do the things you were afraid to do. By pretending to be powerful in the same situation in which you once felt powerless, you break the spell and awaken to your true nature.

3. Make New, Unlimiting Decisions

When you rewrite your past, you also have the opportunity to change the early limiting decisions you made about the nature of your life drama and the role you play in it. By revisiting and recasting meaningful events that once influenced your habitual belief system, you can significantly alter the course of your life. As you revise early decisions so they reflect a more expanded view of what is possible for you in this lifetime, you free yourself to have and enjoy what you really want.

For example, Joni grew up in an impoverished environment with her single mother and three siblings. Often the family lacked food and shelter. Throughout elementary school, Joni recalled feeling ashamed when other children made fun of her tattered, hand-me-down clothes. In adulthood, Joni found herself forever just scraping by financially, no matter how hard she worked to get ahead. By rewriting key scenes from her childhood, Joni was able to reprogram beliefs that she would always have to struggle to make ends meet, and that she was undeserving of financial abundance. As Joni began to make new choices in alignment with her changing attitudes about prosperity, her financial situation improved greatly.

While rewriting past scenes, Joni also began to appreciate some of the positive ways in which her experience of childhood poverty impacted her. She recognized that it made her more compassionate, more resourceful, less judgmental of others, and more willing to lend a helping hand to those in need. She also had become stronger, less concerned about what other people thought of her, and more courageous.

Because revising your habits of thought is so important for awakening from a spellbound state, chapter five focuses exclusively on how to recognize and transform your limiting thoughts and attitudes.

4. Reclaim Lost Parts of the Self

Still another component of rewriting traumatic episodes is finding and reintegrating one's lost parts. As discussed in chapter one, during painful episodes we often lose contact with positive aspects of ourselves. We may forget how to play, or find it impossible to trust another, or feel disconnected from sexual pleasure. When we revisit painful episodes, we have the opportunity to restore our sense of wholeness by accessing and claiming those qualities that have been misplaced in the shadows of our psyches. We can discover a capacity for courage, joy, love, creativity, intimacy, and aliveness that we never realized we possessed.

5. Foster the Development of Fixated Parts

Rewriting the past provides us with the opportunity to nurture and heal the wounded parts of ourselves. As discussed earlier, until these parts are acknowledged and tended to, they may remain frozen at earlier stages of development. This means that while you are spellbound, certain situations will trigger automatic, inappropriate reactions that feel out-of-control and are maladaptive. By offering love, support, and guidance to the hurting child within, you can awaken from your spell and free yourself to respond in more conscious and healthy ways in the present. As the fog lifts, you recognize coping strategies that have been hurting rather than helping you. And you begin to make growth-enhancing choices that enable you to thrive, rather than survive.

Some individuals experience remarkable physical changes as they nurture and heal their wounded selves. One of my clients, a forty-five-year-old mother who had always been relatively flat-chested, found that she literally grew breasts and that her shoulders broadened as she healed from the sexual abuse she endured from ages eight through sixteen. A fifty-three-year-old man reported that he grew chest hair for the first time after healing from childhood abuse. These individuals demonstrate that as we foster emotional development in our previously fixated parts, our arrested physical development may be simultaneously activated.

Exercise eleven will help you to prepare for rewriting scenes by reviewing your notes from earlier exercises.

Exercise #11
Rank-Ordering Your Traumatic Scenes

1. Return now to the notes you made during exercises two and three in chapter two. You should have two lists of past scenes, one for each of the two exercises. The list from exercise two includes events that are related to strong emotional reactions in your present life. The items on the list from exercise three are situations in which you made limiting decisions that impact your thinking today.

2. Imagine a scale from zero to ten, with zero being no emotional charge, or neutral, and ten being a very strong emotional charge. Rate each item from the two lists on the scale from zero to ten. The scenes that have a zero rating should not be at all disturbing to you, while the scenes with a score of ten are highly disturbing.

0		10
neutral		maximum
no disturbance		disturbance

3. List the scenes on each list in rank order, starting with the least disturbing. Some scenes may be grouped together because they are similar traumas that occurred repeatedly over time. For example, if you were sexually abused many times over a period of years, you may choose just one or two representative scenes to put on your list. Rewriting those

94

particular scenes will help you to heal the wounds from the repeated sexual abuse.

4. Put a star next to any scene that appears on more than one list. These may represent traumatic events that seem to be particularly powerful in the negative influence they have upon your life.

Now, review the rank-ordered lists you created in exercise eleven. Choose a scene from either of the two lists, rated between three and five on the zero to ten scale of emotional disturbance. You are now going to have the opportunity to rewrite that memory.

You will need to allow at least thirty minutes for this process. Choose a time when you are certain not to be interrupted. Also, make sure you are in a place where you can speak, yell, or cry in private.

As stated earlier, I recommend that you work with a therapist when doing this process. If you choose to work alone, you may also use the set of compact discs on which I have recorded the exercises from this book, or you may want to tape the instructions for yourself, leaving plenty of long pauses so you can follow along without having to open your eyes and read what to do next.

Exercise #12
Rewriting a Traumatic Memory

1. Make yourself comfortable, close your eyes, take some slow, deep breaths, and imagine you are again in the safety and comfort of your heart sanctuary. Picture it in detail, using all of your senses. Feel its

peace and protection envelop you at every level of your being—mental, physical, spiritual, and emotional. Imagine you are fortifying yourself in order to confront your ghosts when you travel back to the event you have identified.

2. Invite your Spirit to be with you, bathing you in love and support.

3. Going back in your imagination to just minutes before the scene you have identified, find your younger self, and notice everything you can about where he or she is, who else (if anyone) is present, what is happening, and how your younger self is feeling.

4. Next, imagine that your present, adult self steps into the scene, holding the beacon your Inner Being has given you. Tell your younger self who you are, and that you have come to help him or her.

5. Using your imagination, make certain that your adult self is the most powerful force in the scene. You may choose to make yourself ten feet tall, carrying a magical weapon, or picture yourself with divine protection. However you do it is okay, as long as you can feel and be the most powerful person in the scene.

6. As you stand in your power, intervene to protect your younger self in whatever way you wish. Take

this opportunity to tell anyone else present how you feel about what is happening or is about to happen. (Either your younger or older self can do this.) It is best if you actually speak out loud, rather than just in your mind's eye. Know that it is safe for you to express anything you are feeling. The more you are able to access and verbalize all of your emotions, the better. Feel yourself releasing your feelings, once and for all.

7. Next, tell your younger self (out loud) whatever he or she needs to hear to be healed from this event. For example, you may want to say "This was not your fault," or "You didn't deserve to have this happen to you." Promise to always be there to love and protect him or her from now on.

8. You may recognize some limiting decisions that your younger self made during the original event. Here is an opportunity to change those limiting decisions to unlimiting ones. For example, you can change "I am worthless" to "I am worthwhile" by talking (out loud) to your younger self and explaining why it is okay to believe something different now. Think of a whiteboard, with the old belief written on it. Erase it together and, using beautiful colors, write down the new belief.

9. Pretend you are reclaiming anything that was lost or stolen from your younger self during the targeted scene. This will probably be an abstract quality, like

trust in oneself or others, joy, or spontaneity. You can create an object or symbol in your mind's eye that represents the quality you are reclaiming. You may wish to announce to those present in the scene what you are reclaiming and why you are reclaiming it.

10. You can also give back anything to the offender(s) that you do not want. It may be something you have been carrying for all these years, since the traumatic event. For example, you may wish to give back the pain or fear they caused you, or your doubt in your own self-worth.

11. If appropriate, you can rewrite the entire scene from start to finish, righting any wrongs that have been done by you or to you by others. You can create a pretend memory in which everything happens just the way you would have liked for it to happen.

12. Take action to ensure that your younger self is safe and contented. It may feel good to leave your younger self in the new scene you have created. Or, you can imagine you are taking your younger self home with you, or to your heart sanctuary. Do whatever feels best.

13. Shine the light of your beacon on the scene and notice how you are able to see through the illusions, and recognize the truth of this situation. Identify any ways in which this event helped to make you a better person. What are the positive

qualities you developed as a result of this life experience? Allow yourself to experience gratitude for
these.

14. Slowly and gradually come back to the present.

The goal is to use the process outlined above to rewrite several of
the traumatic scenes you have listed and rank-ordered in exercise
eleven. Begin by rewriting those scenes that have a lower ranking
on the one to ten scale of disturbance, and gradually introduce
scenes that received higher rankings. Scenes you starred are particularly important to rewrite.

You may find that after rewriting one representative scene,
that the emotional charge is gone from other, similar memories as
well. For example, if you remember many times you were called
"stupid" by members of your family, it may only be necessary to
rewrite one particularly memorable incident, in order to receive
optimal benefits. As you work on that one event, others, which
are similar, may also lose their negative hold on you.

Rosa Releases Her Phantoms

The following case example illustrates how rewriting a traumatic
scene can help us awaken from a spellbound state and restore our
emotional vitality.

Rosa is a bright, attractive young woman who has years of
experience working in a busy airport as a reservations agent. Rosa
sought my assistance following a distressing incident in which an
angry older male customer began to scream at her that she was an
"incompetent idiot." The harder she tried to help the man, the
louder and more unruly he became. Even his wife tried to calm

him down, but to no avail. Normally, Rosa is able to deal with the most difficult customers in a calm, polite, and professional manner. But in this situation, she found herself trembling, paralyzed with fear, and unable to take appropriate action. As co-workers came to her aide, she burst into tears and ran back to the employee break room. There, she continued crying and shaking uncontrollably for many hours. The next day, she was overcome with anxiety any time she saw a man who even slightly resembled the one who had yelled at her.

In my office, Rosa explained that terrible things had happened in her childhood, which she had just tried to block out. We decided to see if ghosts from her past were creating a spellbound reaction in the present. Under my direction, Rosa closed her eyes, relaxed, and then identified the feelings in her body associated with the man's verbal attack. We then traced those feelings back to another time and place when she felt the same feelings in her body. Rosa immediately began to cry, as she described a familiar scene from her early years in which her father was violently beating her mother, after Rosa's mother had simply offered him something to eat.

We rewrote the scene by having Rosa's present, empowered, adult self step into the scene (before the violence began) and prevent her father from hitting her mother. After letting little Rosa know she was there to help her, adult Rosa threatened to call the police and have her father taken off to jail if he laid a hand on her mother. Then she told him how his past behavior had affected her. She expressed her anger, hurt, confusion, and hatred toward him for the countless incidents of abuse she had witnessed against her mother. Finally, she banished him from the house forever.

Rosa then loved and nurtured her younger self, telling her the things she most needed to hear. Lastly, she addressed her mother, expressing her love, and saying how sorry she was to see her mother allow herself to be the victim of her father's abuse.

Next, we returned to the present, and Rosa rewrote the scene at work (in her mind's eye) with the verbally abusive customer to reflect the way she would have liked to handle it.

When Rosa opened her eyes, she reported feeling tired but good, lighter, and clearer. She explained to me that her mother eventually had found the courage to take her five children and leave her violent husband. We talked about the positive qualities Rosa developed as a result of what she experienced in her childhood: strength, closeness with her siblings, compassion, and determination to have a loving and harmonious marriage (which she does) and to be a great parent (which she is)!

The following week, Rosa returned to report that she was feeling great, with more energy than usual, and a pervasive sense that something had been lifted. What's more, the abusive man had returned to her workstation, and Rosa was able to deal with him appropriately, without having any emotional reaction triggered within her. To her surprise, she found herself feeling sorry for him and his wife. And she no longer felt anxious when she spotted a man who resembled the offensive customer.

Rosa's report is typical for those who have rewritten a key traumatic scene. Most say they feel clearer, lighter, and as if something has been lifted from them. Although people usually feel very tired at the end of the session, a few days later they often experience a new supply of energy and vitality. They experience how good it feels to break the ghosts' spell and become fully alive again.

CHAPTER FIVE
REVISING THOUGHTS AND ATTITUDES

One of the chief ways the ghosts maintain their control over you is by infiltrating your thoughts and distorting your perceptions. To awaken from your phantom-induced trance you must remove your spellbound lenses by shifting habitual ways of thinking, so you are controlling your mind, rather than allowing your mind to control you. You needn't permit the ghosts to imprison you for one more moment with doubts about your worth, your power, and your potential to create the kind of life you truly desire. You can begin today to use the potency of your thoughts and beliefs to transform your life in profound ways that are in alignment with your fondest hopes and dreams.

Characteristics of Spellbound Thinking

In order to change spellbound thinking, we first have to recognize it. Since our haunted thoughts often happen beneath our conscious awareness, let us review their typical characteristics.

Spellbound Thinking Is Repetitive, Automatic, and Self-Hypnotic

Often we are so accustomed to our spellbound thinking that we fail to recognize we are playing the same destructive tapes in our heads, over and over again. The messages are so familiar that we don't stop to question their validity or to push the "off" button. We tell ourselves "I'm so inadequate," "No one would ever want to have a relationship with me," or "I can't do anything right." And these thoughts appear to be beyond our control.

Because of the repetitive nature of our ghost-induced thinking, it operates as a kind of self-hypnosis. If you tell yourself hundreds of times every day for years that you just can't do math, then guess what? You can't! The best teachers in the world can't overcome that kind of mental programming!

One woman who wanted to lose weight but had been unsuccessful for years "caught" herself telling herself how fat she was hundreds of times every day. Finally, she realized that if she was to be successful in losing weight, it was essential that she stop "feeding" herself these negative messages, which were a form of self-hypnosis that actually worked against her weight-loss efforts.

Spellbound Thinking Is Negative, Judgmental, and Catastrophic

Spellbound thoughts are rejecting, self-destructive, self-sabotaging, and limiting. They tell us we can't do the good things we want to do without dire consequences. "If I take that class, I'll fail and everyone will know how incompetent I am." "If I try out for that play, I will forget my lines and look like a fool." "If I ask that person on a date then I will be rejected because I am not good enough." "If I quit my job, no one else will hire me because I am too old."

People and circumstances are viewed through our spellbound lenses in the worst possible light. If there is a possible down side to any situation, our ghosts will focus on that. The most joyful events can be turned into a source of pain. The greatest success will be perceived as an utter failure. The most incredible opportunity will be viewed as a set-up for disaster.

Since our world view is problem-focused, we give primary attention to our own difficulties and to those of others. Life becomes a series of painful predicaments to be dealt with. Since we identify with the trials and tribulations we have endured, and use them as the basis for our self-definition, we become afraid of life without our problems, uncertain of who we would be without them.

Our spellbound thoughts are often catastrophic, jumping to conclusions that one bump in the road means the end of the road. If one person rejects us, then we tell ourselves that everyone will. If we get one poor grade on a test, then we will never pass the class. If we experience an unfamiliar pain, we are dying.

Spellbound thinking seduces us with judgments, generally that we are "better than" or "less than" others. "I'm a loser," or "I'm smarter than him" are two sides of the same coin. As long as we are comparing ourselves to someone else to determine who is smarter, better looking, more successful, or more talented, we are under the spell of our phantoms.

Spellbound Thinking Keeps Us Stuck
Regretting the Past or Worrying about the Future

As long as we are under the spell of our ghosts, we are missing out on the present moments of our lives. As discussed in chapter three, our phantoms prefer that we are ruminating about what did or didn't happen in the past, or worrying about what might happen in the future. Our spellbound thoughts dredge up unhappy events from the past that make us feel guilty, sad, angry, or regretful, and replay them over and over again. Or, they may fast-forward our minds to a future in which we envision dire consequence coming to pass, evoking feelings of anxiety and fear. All the while, we are distracted from the feeling of well-being that is always available to us in the now.

Note that recalling a pleasant memory or dreaming of something wonderful to come is not a form of spellbound thinking.

There is nothing wrong with dwelling on past delights or future pleasures—one may even use such thoughts as a way of keeping one's ghosts at bay. It is only when we focus on the unpleasant past or anticipate an awful future that we are under the spell of our phantoms.

Spellbound Thinking Makes Us Feel Terrible

The best way to know if the ghosts have infiltrated your thoughts is to notice how you feel. Spellbound thinking will always make you feel terrible, whether invoking feelings of depression, anger, frustration, guilt, shame, hopelessness, hurt, or fear. Negative emotions are a helpful signal from your Spirit that you are engaging in harmful habits of thought. Your feelings can be your best guide in identifying the negative thoughts you wish to change, and in monitoring your progress as you shift your beliefs from limiting to unlimiting ones.

While we often believe that our negative emotions are triggered by events in our lives, actually they are a by-product of the things we tell ourselves about the events in our lives. For example, when Steve didn't get the job for which he had interviewed, he felt defeated, hopeless, and depressed. These feelings however, were due to the messages he was giving himself, like "No one will ever hire me," and "I didn't get this job because I'm not as good as the other people who applied for it." Although it is natural for Steve to feel some disappointment under the circumstances, he was making himself feel even worse by engaging in catastrophic thinking.

Instead of thinking that this one, failed attempt to get hired means he will *never* get hired, Steve could remind himself that this interview was good practice, and that the right job will come along for him if he remains open to it. He might also tell himself that he probably didn't get this job because it wasn't the right or best one for him.

Removing Your Spellbound Lenses

Although it may feel as though your thoughts are automatic and outside the realm of your control, this is far from the truth. You have ultimate control over your thoughts, and if you desire, you can even change patterns of thought that have been familiar to you for a very long time. It may be challenging at first, but if you are determined to think differently, you can and will. Be prepared to reap wonderful rewards as you choose new places to direct your attention.

Begin by Becoming Conscious of Your Thoughts and Speech

Begin to notice your repetitive thought patterns. Do you focus more on your positive or your negative attributes? Are you more likely to pay attention to what's right, or what's wrong in your world? Do you tend to dwell on thoughts of appreciation, joy, and delightful anticipation, or on problems, misfortune, and doom and gloom? Do you speak more of others' assets or their shortcomings? Do you recall your most satisfying memories, or ruminate on past "failures?" Are you more likely to see the glass as half empty or half full? Do you spend more time thinking about what you want, or what you don't want?

Pay Attention to How You Are Feeling

As stated above, your emotions give you immediate feedback regarding the kind of thoughts you are entertaining, and whether or not your negative mind is running the show. If you are feeling uplifted, joyful, peaceful, appreciative, passionate, or hopeful, then you are holding positive thoughts, and you are connected to your spiritual source. If however, you are feeling sad, scared, anxious, resentful, regretful or angry, then your thoughts are most likely "on automatic" and playing an old tape.

Begin to monitor your feelings throughout the day. Ask yourself "What am I feeling right now? Am I feeling good or bad?" Your answers will enable you to recognize if and when the ghosts have taken over. And if they have, you can take immediate action to disempower them.

Think of a Thought That Feels Better

When you become aware that you are feeling bad, and therefore, engaging in spellbound thinking, you need only find a new thought that feels better to you in the moment. For example, if you are thinking about an upcoming test and feeling anxious as you entertain thoughts of failing it, you may choose to tell yourself things like, "I am well-prepared for this exam. I have done well on other, similar tests, so I am capable of doing well on this one. I believe I deserve to pass."

It is important that whatever you tell yourself makes you feel better. Simply repeating empty words is not helpful, if they do not make a difference in how you are feeling.

If you cannot think of a thought about the same subject that feels better to you, then you can either focus your mind on a completely different subject that makes you feel good—such as something you appreciate, or something that brings you joy—or you can do something that helps you to feel peaceful, like meditation or guided visualization.

Awakening from your spell means stopping the thoughts that are making you feel bad, and replacing them with something else that helps you to lighten-up.

Replace Worries with Positive Outcomes

When we worry, we forecast the worst about the future. Rather than helping us, worries make it more likely that things will turn out badly. The best thing to do when you catch yourself worrying about what could go wrong, is to choose to entertain thoughts of things going better than ever. For example, if you are worried about growing older and weaker, imagine instead feeling stronger and more capable as you age. If you fear getting sick, picture your immune system functioning at optimal levels. Should you dread giving a speech, imagine thundering applause following your splendid performance.

Focus on What You Want

Still another way to awaken from your ghost-induced trance, is by shifting your attention from things you don't want to things you do want. Our phantoms encourage us to pay the most attention to those things in our lives that are wrong, bad, or missing, rather than those things that are right, good, and present. We are seduced into focusing more on our liabilities, than our assets. We complain about what isn't working in our lives, and remain oblivious to what is working in our lives. We zero in on our partner's faults and ignore their best attributes. And we put our deficiencies under a microscope, while being blind to our greatest gifts.

Whatever we focus on in our lives increases. The more we focus on what we don't want, the worse it gets. Conversely, the more we focus on what we do want, the better it gets.

Just by beginning to give your attention to what's right in your life, you can begin to transform it in positive ways.

Your Attitude Makes All the Difference

Often I see people who are convinced they cannot or should not hold a more positive attitude until people or things around them have changed. They feel legitimate in their resentments, complaints, and unhappiness, and point to circumstances outside of themselves as justification for their negative reactions. Unfortunately, these individuals are allowing something out of their control to disturb their sense of well-being. If we look for it, there will always be something we can find in our lives that we can use as an excuse for not feeling good in the moment. What's more, those situations that bother us most are not likely to improve until we become more positively focused.

If you are waiting for everything in your life to be "perfect" in order to feel and be positive, then you are doomed to a life of unhappiness. But your life will become better and better as you focus more on what you want, and less on what you don't want. Real changes happen from the inside out.

The following process will help you to refocus your attention on what is right in your life.

Exercise #13
Focusing on the Good in Your Life

1. Choose a day, and see how many good things you can notice and acknowledge to yourself during that day. Try to notice things you normally take for granted or ignore. Pretend you are experiencing everything for the first time. Notice everything and everyone that is a positive in your life. Notice your own good qualities. Notice the things that go well that day. Pay attention to the little things, like the way the clouds look in the sky, the smile of a friend,

the feeling of warm water washing over you in the shower, the smell of coffee brewing, or the sound of a favorite song on the radio. Be aware of the feelings of well-being these things create.

Identifying Thought Traps

Besides dealing with our thoughts on a day-to-day and moment-by-moment basis, releasing our past means going within and changing those early limiting decisions we made during traumatic moments of our lives, in order to become less vulnerable to thought traps. Chapter four described how you can use the process of rewriting a past scene to revise early limiting decisions. What follows are additional instructions for recognizing and transforming your habitual negative thoughts.

Since most of us tend to think that our limiting beliefs are simply accurate depictions of "reality," sometimes they manage to elude us in spite of our best efforts to unmask them. As we gaze at ourselves and others through our distorted, spellbound lenses, we believe we are seeing things clearly, as they really are. Our lenses show us a "reality" that is in perfect agreement with our habitual thought patterns. For example, Margo believed that all men are insensitive jerks. When she encountered men who did not fit her stereotype, she either didn't notice them, or she would misinterpret even the kindest gesture on their part as mean or insensitive. Hence, Margo's distorted lenses reinforce her negative attitudes about men, and cause her to confuse her limiting thinking with "the truth" about men. Since our lenses always distort reality according to what we expect to see, each of us sees our own unique version of "the truth" about ourselves, others, and events in our lives.

Next you have the opportunity to identify a habitual thought pattern that may be blocking the attainment of a particular goal.

Exercise #14
Working with a Goal

1. Think of a specific goal that you would like to accomplish. This can be anything that is important to you, like finding a life partner, enjoying greater financial success, mastering a sport, accessing greater creativity, or improving your health.

2. Form a brief, positive, present-tense sentence stating that you are now accomplishing or have accomplished the goal you have specified. For example, "I am now enjoying perfect health." Write it at the top of a piece of paper.

3. On the front of the paper, write all of the reasons you would like to have this thing, why you believe it is possible, and why you deserve to have it.

4. On the back of the paper, write down any reasons why you might not be able to attain this goal, *even if another part of you says they are not reasonable*. If you are fearful about having something you want, write down your worst possible fears. Again, don't be concerned if there is another part of you that does not have these fears. Write down all of the reasons why it may not be possible to have this

thing you want. Put down anything that occurs to you. Finally, write down all of the reasons why you might not deserve to have it. Be honest with yourself, even if a more optimistic part of you disagrees with what you are writing down.

5. When you are done, this list represents the limiting attitudes that may be blocking you from the accomplishment of your specified goal. The next part of this chapter will instruct you in how to transform these negative thought patterns into positive ones. The front side of the page represents all of the positive thoughts and attitudes you already hold about this goal. You can strengthen these by thinking about them and repeating them to yourself often, as you joyfully fantasize about the accomplishment of your goal.

Activating New Beliefs

In some cases, you may wish to train yourself to replace your negative beliefs with positive ones. This means you consciously and deliberately decide to establish new habits of thinking that are more in alignment with how you want your life to be. These are some steps you can take to train yourself to think in more optimistic ways.

1. Decide what you want to believe.

Create brief, positive, present-tense sentences, called *affirmations*, to replace a limiting belief that you wish to change. When using an affirmation you state what you would like to believe about yourself or your life, as if you already believe it.

Pay close attention to how you feel as you say or write a particular affirmation. You should feel uplifted, hopeful, or encouraged as you say your affirmation. If repeating a particular affirmation only makes you feel worse instead of better, or if you feel nothing at all as you say it, then find another sentence that has a more positive effect on you.

For example, Emma wanted to change the habitual thought that she would never find someone to love her. She began to tell herself "I have a wonderful life partner," but found that those words just made her feel worse about being alone. Emma found that when she told herself, "I have many friends who love me," and "I have a lot to offer in a relationship" and "I deserve to have a loving partner," she felt uplifted and optimistic about her future. This was a signal that these affirmations were the right ones for her to be using at the time.

Affirmations

In chapter two, we reviewed ten common thought traps. Let's look at some affirmations you can use to replace these negative habits of thought.

"I am unworthy."

- I am worthy.
- I deserve the best that life has to offer.
- I deserve (love, relaxation, financial abundance, success, joy, good health, etc.).
- I now open to receive my highest good.
- I am worthy of having and enjoying what I desire.

"I am not good enough."

- I am good enough.
- I love and accept myself exactly as I am.
- My belief in myself grows stronger every day.
- I surround myself with people who believe in me.
- I am brimming with confidence in my ability to accomplish my goals.
- It is easy for me to recognize and acknowledge my strengths.

"It is essential that everyone else approve of me."

- I release the need for others to approve of me.
- I now find the courage, strength, and confidence to act in accordance with my inner guidance.

"I am powerless."

- I now create my life just as I want it to be.
- I exercise my personal power by making healthy choices.
- I embrace my power to make a positive difference.
- I am capable of doing anything I set my mind to doing.
- Today I awaken fully to my beauty, power, and greatest potential.

"I cannot trust myself."

- It is easy for me to trust and follow my inner guidance.
- I trust myself to know what is best for me.
- I open to perfect guidance from my Enlightened Spirit.
- I joyfully and courageously follow my dreams.

"I cannot trust other people."

- I only attract people who treat me
  with respect and loving-kindness.
- I surround myself with people who are trustworthy.
- I choose friends and lovers who are worthy of my trust.
- I let love in.
- I easily notice the beauty in others.

"There is not enough."

- I live in an abundant Universe.
- I now have all of the (time, money, love, success, joy,
  friendships, creativity) I desire.
- Blessings are flowing into my life in unlimited quantities.
- I am now open to receive an unlimited supply of
  (money, love, success, joy, friendships, creativity).

"Life is a struggle."

- Good things come easily to me now.
- I attract my highest good easily and joyfully.
- I release the need to struggle.
- I surrender to my highest good now.

"It is not safe for me to be myself."

- I now find the courage and confidence to be my true self.
- I joyfully honor and express my uniqueness.
- I live in accordance with my inner truth and wisdom.

"I am responsible for everyone else's happiness."

- I empower others to be responsible for themselves.
- I take responsibility for my physical, mental,
  emotional, and Spiritual well-being.
- I take good care of myself.

2. Establish the intention to release the old belief and embrace the new one.

Once you have identified one or more affirmations that feel good, the next step is to be very clear with yourself that you intend to release the old way of thinking and to replace it with the new attitude. There is tremendous power in establishing a clear intention. Your intention represents a strong desire that you are using to fuel the engine of change. It is a signal for all of your internal resources to align and assist you in the accomplishment of your objective.

3. Speak your affirmations, and write them down.

Begin to state the new belief to yourself many times daily, and write it down, giving it your full attention as you do so. Make it your personal mantra. Any time you catch yourself thinking in the old way, replace it with your new affirmation. Here you are using repetition as a form of self-hypnosis, so the more often you repeat your affirmation, the better—as long as it feels uplifting to say it.

4. Look for evidence in your life that your new belief is true.

Consciously and deliberately keep an eye out for circumstances that validate your new belief. Look for signs that your new way of thinking is in alignment with "reality." For example, if you are affirming your good health, take note of each period of time when you are pain-free or feeling more energized. See how much evidence of your improved health you can compile every day.

Your ghosts will want to provide you with evidence that your old way of thinking is "true." For example, if you are affirming that you are healthier, they will want to draw your attention to any indicators of pain or disease, and attempt to convince you that your physical health is deteriorating, rather than improving. They will even remind you of past bodily conditions that got worse, not better. Your challenge is to ignore your phantoms, and to seek out evidence to support your new way of thinking. It is present if you look for it.

Be sure to recall experiences from your past that are in alignment with your new belief. Our tendency is to forget about life events that do not fit our current view of reality. It is likely that you have already had certain experiences in the distant or recent past that can be used to reinforce your new way of seeing things. For example, if you are affirming that you are perfectly healthy, remember times when you were vibrantly alive. Recall some specific memories associated with your physical body's optimal state of wellness and vitality, focusing on what it felt like. Allow yourself to re-experience that state of being.

Each time you seek evidence to support your new belief, you are seeing right through the illusions cast by your phantoms. The more you notice good things in your life, the more you awaken from your spellbound state.

5. Activate the power of pretend.

A powerful way to adopt a new, unlimiting belief is to pretend that you already believe it. As you go about your daily life, act as if you already hold your affirmation as the absolute truth. For example, if you want to believe that you can trust yourself, pretend that you already do. Throughout the day, ask yourself, "How would I behave in this situation if I trusted myself?" As you try out new ways of behaving, see yourself as pretending to play a new role in your own life.

Sometimes it helps to think of another person—either someone you know or someone you know of—who appears to have the qualities, lifestyle, and attitude you desire. As you go about your day, pretend to be that person. When you are faced with challenging situations, ask yourself how that person would view the situation, and how he or she would most likely handle it. By pretending to be someone else, you can discover strengths you didn't know you have, and try out a new repertoire of behaviors.

6. Rewrite the traumatic scenes in which you first adopted or strengthened the limiting belief.

In past chapters we discussed how limiting thought patterns are established when we make decisions during traumatic moments of our lives. You can use exercise three in chapter two to trace a particular negative belief and identify those scenes when you first adopted it, and then reinforced or strengthened it. Changing your mind is one of the most powerful ways to alter your early decisions. You can refer to exercise twelve in chapter four to guide you through this process.

Before rewriting the scenes, write down the new, unlimiting decisions you want your younger self to make. During step eight (in exercise twelve), you will assist your younger self in adopting the new way of thinking. Then you can rewrite the entire scene in your imagination so that everything happens in accordance with your new decision.

7. Play with your imagination.

In addition to rewriting past scenes, you can use your imagination to become more familiar with how it feels to hold your new belief. The more comfortable you are envisioning your new life, the more quickly it will become a part of your reality. Use the following exercise as a springboard for playing with your imagination.

119

Exercise #15
Using Your Imagination to Change a Belief

1. Begin by putting your body in a comfortable position, closing your eyes, and breathing deeply. Imagine yourself again in the safety, calm and comfort of your heart sanctuary. Use all of your senses to fill in the details of what it is like there.

2. Imagine that your Spirit is present, offering you love, wisdom, and support. Think about the new, unlimiting belief you want to fully accept. Pretend that your Inner Being offers you a symbol that represents that new belief. Experience the symbol as pulsating with life, radiant with light, and very beautiful.

3. See yourself taking the symbol from your Spirit, and placing it in your heart. Feel its uplifting, beautiful energy spreading to every part of you.

4. Imagine that as the symbol's light spreads, your new belief is being encoded in the DNA of each cell of your being. Know that your new way of thinking is now an integral part of you.

5. Imagine you are stepping into a brand new reality, in which your new, positive belief is reflected all about you. Pretend your life is like a movie, the most wonderful, satisfying, joyful, fulfilling movie you have ever seen. Make it as real as you can. Fill

it in with lots of details. Get excited about what you are experiencing. Be playful. Think big. What is your life like? What does it feel like to live in this brand new reality? What are you able to do now that you weren't able to do before? Feel yourself adjusting to this new reality, becoming comfortable with it, until it feels very natural to you.

6. Stay in this new place for as long as you like. Whenever you are ready, come back feeling clear-headed, refreshed and alert.

7. Do this guided meditation often, until your new reality is as familiar to you as your "real" life.

How Long Will It Take?

It is normal to get caught up in the question of how long it will take for positive changes to manifest. But try to put this question aside, and just be open to the joyous opportunities and wonderful life blessings when they present themselves. When we begin counting the minutes since we adopted new thoughts and attitudes, we prepare the soil for our ghosts to plant seeds of doubt in our consciousness. What's more, we are again focusing our attention on what we don't want (no change), rather than what we do want (change). It is important to avoid thinking that our lives must be transformed according to a particular timeline. Trust instead that things will happen when it is best for you. Know that as you continue to practice your new habits of thought, positive changes will come at exactly the right time and place.

121

CHAPTER SIX
REALIZING FORGIVENESS

Forgiveness is the most powerful medicine you possess for healing body, mind, and Spirit. It is the ultimate cure for whatever ails you. The light of forgiveness transforms everything it touches. Forgiveness opens the door to miracles in your life. It frees your Spirit to soar and invites your heart to sing.

Forgiveness is the last step in breaking free from your past. In fact, all of the processes described in chapters three through five are preparation for the final act of forgiving yourself and others. When you forgive, you hand your ghosts their official eviction notice. Until you forgive, you may do a great job of gaining control over your inner tormentors, but it takes forgiveness to dispel them once and for all.

What does it mean to forgive? To forgive is to let go. When you forgive, you completely release whatever negative thoughts or feelings you have been holding toward your self or another person. You say goodbye to hate, resentment, anger, hurt, guilt, and shame. You stop ruminating about how you would like to see the other punished. You cease replaying the details of the traumatic episode, telling yourself "If only..." Forgiveness is a powerful choice you make in order to be whole again.

Forgiving Yourself

Often it is hardest to forgive ourselves. I have seen many clients who have easily pardoned family, friends, and strangers for any and all deliberate and unintended transgressions. They don't hold grudges against another living soul. Yet, they have refused to grant themselves the same compassion that they offer so freely to others. Instead, they keep a long mental list of their own "mistakes" and use it to torment themselves. With prodding from their ghosts, they criticize themselves from morning till night. "I should have known better." "I shouldn't have let that happen." "I should have dealt differently with that situation." They judge themselves harshly and heap upon themselves daily portions of guilt and shame. They use their mistakes as justification for the belief that they are worthless and do not deserve to be happy.

Nothing you have done is unforgivable. You are human, and by nature, humans make mistakes. Mistakes are how we learn. Mistakes are how we become better people. In having done things you regret, you are no different than any other person on this planet. You are not here this lifetime to suffer in payment for past errors. Your mistakes make you wiser and more compassionate. They enable you to make better choices the next time, gain humility, and open your heart to the foibles and frailties of others.

You cannot release the ghosts that haunt you until you grant yourself the same mercy you have granted others. Until you forgive yourself, your life remains on hold. As long as you maintain stockpiles of guilt, shame, and self-blame, you are destined to remain stuck in the past and vulnerable to the influence of your phantoms. One client, Michael, had been suffering from depression and an addiction to painkillers for nine years. He was barely sustaining his business, and living a lonely and sad existence in a small, dingy apartment. During therapy, I learned that Michael had never forgiven himself for an argument he had with his teenaged son the night before his son died in a freak swimming accident. Even prescription drugs could not kill the pain of the guilt and self-blame he carried with him. Michael's miserable life was in alignment with his belief that he deserved to be punished for his perceived wrongdoing. Nothing in Michael's world would change until he decided that he didn't need to suffer any longer. Michael was desperately in need of the most powerful painkiller of all—a generous dose of self-forgiveness.

Self-Acceptance Is the Most Important Ingredient

To forgive yourself is to release the negative judgments you have been fostering about yourself, that you are bad, stupid, shameful, disgraceful, or guilty, and replace them with self-acceptance. While negative self-judgment prevents you from moving forward, self-acceptance invites personal growth. Acknowledging your mistakes and shortcomings in an open and non-critical fashion is a major step in our spiritual development.

Of course, the ghosts warn us that if we accept ourselves, we won't learn from our mistakes. This is the illusion. Continuing to suffer from something we did or didn't do years ago is not learning from the past. It is using the past as an excuse for not being fully alive in the present.

Only when we stop berating ourselves about what lies behind us, can we lift the spell cast by our inner phantoms. Fairy tales abound with messages about the power of love and acceptance to awaken us from our spellbound state. Both Snow White and Sleeping Beauty are ultimately awakened from their deep sleep when kissed by a prince. These stories remind us that through self-acceptance, we can resuscitate ourselves, restore our vitality and rediscover our zest for life.

Exercise #16
Compiling a Self-Forgiveness List

1. Make a list of all the things for which you have not yet forgiven yourself. Be honest with yourself. What do you still feel guilty, ashamed, or sorry about? What are you angry with yourself about? Do you berate yourself for something you did or did not do in the past? What do you most regret?

2. Rank order your list according to how distressing each item is for you. List items from the least distressing to the most distressing.

3. For each item, write down all of the things you have learned from the experience. How did it make you a better person? How are you different today, as a result of the experience?

Next, choose something on your list that you are ready to heal and release. You can use the following process to forgive yourself and let go of the past.

Exercise #17
Forgiving Yourself

1. Close your eyes, take a few deep breaths, and picture yourself in the peace, comfort, and beauty of your heart sanctuary. Use your senses to fill in all of the details of that sacred, inner space.

2. Picture your younger self in a past scene or situation for which you would now like to forgive yourself. Recall the scene as vividly as you can in your mind's eye. Engage all of your senses. The scene you imagine may be representative of a series of events.

3. Take the perspective of your younger self in that scene. Recall how it felt to be your younger self in the situation you are recreating in your mind's eye.

4. Imagine that your present-day self steps into the scene. View your younger, less-developed self through eyes of wisdom, understanding and compassion.

5. Tell your younger self out loud that you are choosing to forgive him or her for the choices he or she made. Explain how his or her mistakes enabled you to learn and grow. Express your willingness to let go of negative judgments and painful emotions you have harbored against your younger self.

6. Feel yourself becoming lighter and freer as you release all of the negativity you have been carrying regarding your younger self in this situation. Feel your heart overflowing with love for your younger self. Acknowledge his or her inherent beauty and goodness.

7. If you wish, you can rewrite the entire scene, imagining everything the way you would have liked for it to have been.

8. When you are ready, return to this time and place feeling clear-headed and alert, knowing that you have taken an important step in your own healing.

Use this process for each of the items that you listed in exercise seventeen. Repeat this exercise as many times as you need to for each item, until you have forgiven yourself completely.

Forgiving Others

Many people hold misconceptions about forgiving others that make it difficult for them to take advantage of this potent medicine. Let's look at seven common myths about forgiveness.

Myth #1
"The other person has to do something before I can forgive him or her."

Sometimes we don't forgive someone because we are waiting for the other to ask for forgiveness, express remorse, take responsibility for bad behavior, or make restitution. This is the equivalent of putting the power to heal yourself in the hands of the person who has ostensibly wronged you. You may spend the rest of your life waiting for this other person to change, all the while suffering the consequences of carrying your ghosts to your grave.

Similarly, a person need not be present in order for you to forgive him or her. Forgiveness is an inside job; it is not necessary for you to communicate with the person you are choosing to forgive.

Your healing need not be in any way controlled by what someone else does or doesn't do. You can choose to forgive another at any time, regardless of whether that person ever sees the light. You have the power to let go of the past and to set yourself free.

Myth #2
"If I forgive, I'm saying that what the other person did was okay."

Forgiveness does not send the message that another's bad behavior was okay. For example, when we forgive someone who abused us, we aren't saying that it was fine for that person to treat us that way. Rather, we are saying that we are not going to continue to dwell on the past and carry the heavy feelings associated with the abuse. When we lighten our emotional load the abuser cannot continue to torment us in the present.

Myth #3
"I must hold positive feelings for the person I am forgiving."

Forgiving another does not necessarily mean replacing the negative feelings you have held with positive ones. When Sara forgave the stranger who brutally raped her, it did not mean she was suddenly overcome with love for him. It did mean she was no longer going to hold on to the hatred, rage, pain, and shame that had been triggered by the attack. Forgiveness does not require placing the other in a positive light. Rather, it is the release of the negative energy you have been carrying toward the offending party.

Forgiveness may help us to access love for another that has been buried under the pain. Often, the people we love the most are the ones we have the hardest time forgiving. However, forgiving is not contingent upon our being willing or able to love the person who has harmed us.

In some cases, as we forgive, our hurt and anger melt into compassion for the other person. No one hurts another individual unless he or she is also in emotional pain. Sometimes as we forgive, we are able to recognize the unhealed wounds of the person who harmed us. Although this doesn't make the other person's behavior acceptable, it does make it easier to forgive when we understand that the other is also under the destructive influence of ghosts from the past.

Myth #4
"Forgiveness is something I do for the other."

Forgiving someone else is a gift you give yourself. It takes a lot of your energy to continue to hold on to negative feelings toward another person. Forgiveness releases this energy so you can apply it to more constructive and joyful pursuits.

Harboring bitterness, resentment, hatred, or ill-will toward another is one of the most damaging things you can do to yourself. These negative emotions can poison your being, weaken your immune system, and ultimately make you sick. You needn't give someone else the power to impact your life in such profoundly destructive ways.

Letting go of your negative feelings about another person is a powerful choice you can make for your own health and well-being. Forgiving someone is one of the best things you can do for you.

Myth #5
"If I forgive, I may get hurt again."

Forgiving another does not mean forgetting the things the experience has taught you. If someone badly mistreats you, forgiving that person does not mean you give that person the opportunity to hurt you again. It only means you are not going to carry the pain or bitterness with you any longer. You can forgive the past, while holding on to its valuable lessons. Forgiving doesn't mean you are naive or unwilling to set appropriate boundaries with others. It does mean you keep the wisdom you have acquired while releasing the undesirable emotions you've accumulated along the way.

Myth #6
"I only need to forgive someone once."

Forgiveness is a process that takes time. You may need to forgive someone daily for months until it feels as if you have really let go once and for all. Be gentle with yourself if you find that the negative feelings pop up again when you thought you had released them. Just affirm once more to yourself that you are choosing to let go of those feelings.

Myth #7
"I need to understand why someone did what he or she did before I can forgive that person."

Needing to know why someone acted badly before forgiving that individual can be a dangerous trap. Life is filled with mysteries. Often we never know the true origins of another's behavior. To think that we need to understand before we can forgive is to remain stuck in the past for the rest of our days. You don't need to know why a person acted as he or she did in order to forgive and move on.

The Power of Forgiveness

When Tom came to see me, he was furious with his ex-wife, Lori, and had been battling with her for a year over who would keep their family home. Tom resented Lori for ending the marriage, and putting him and their two sons through a painful divorce. He believed that since she had chosen to leave him for another man, he should be permitted to move back into their home while Lori found another place to live.

Tom was tired of feeling so angry and unhappy all the time. He also realized that his bitterness toward Lori was not helpful to their children. During one session, he decided that he wanted to forgive

Lori, give her the house, and move on with his life. That evening, as he enjoyed his evening run on the beach, Tom spoke to Lori in his mind's eye, telling her that he was letting go of all bad feelings toward her and releasing the house to her as well. He was instantly overcome with a feeling of lightness and a surge of positive energy. By the time he arrived home from his run, he felt at peace within, and really good about himself and the choice he had made to forgive Lori. He noticed that the answering machine was blinking—a call had come in during his run. To his astonishment, it was Lori, saying, "Tom, I have decided that you can have the house!"

Exercise #18
Creating a Forgiveness List

1. Make a list of all of the people you believe you need to forgive. Be honest with yourself. Include anyone toward whom you feel bitter, resentful, or spiteful, or anyone you feel has hurt you deeply.

For the following exercise, have one person in mind whom you are ready to forgive.

Exercise #19
The Rainbow Bridge

1. Close your eyes, and picture yourself in the serenity, safety and comfort of your heart sanctuary. Breathe deeply, relaxing more and more completely with every breath.

2. Imagine that you can see a magnificent rainbow, extending from your heart sanctuary up into the heavens. The colors of the rainbow are bright, clear, and radiant.

3. You notice the rainbow is a bridge you can walk on. If you choose, you can go now slowly to the center of the bridge, where you will meet face-to-face with the person you want to forgive. Note that you are completely safe and protected while on this bridge. No one can harm you.

4. You may notice yourself viewing this person through the wise eyes of your Enlightened Spirit, or accessing the compassion your Greater Self feels for this individual. Perhaps you become aware of the beauty of this person's Spiritual Essence. Or you may suddenly have a clear picture of the wounded child within this person.

5. Take time to tell this person that you are choosing to forgive him or her. Explain what feelings or judgments you have been holding on to, and why you are choosing to let them go. As you speak, the other person may only listen. If you wish, you can ask the other to respond to you when you are finished, or engage in a dialogue. Feel yourself releasing all of the emotional baggage you have been carrying around as you talk to this person.

6. As you finish speaking, a brilliant stream of pure, up-lifting, healing light enters your head and torso and dissolves any remnants of pain, anger, hatred, or resentment that you are still holding against this individual. Notice how light and free you feel.

7. Do whatever feels good to end this encounter, and return to your heart sanctuary. Come back to this time and place whenever you are ready, feeling clear-headed and alert.

Repeat this process as often as necessary. See if you can meet each person you wish to forgive on the rainbow bridge at least once.

Celebrating Forgiveness

We use rituals, or ceremonies, to mark life's transitions. Some common rituals in western cultures include baptisms, marriages, funerals, and birthday parties. During rituals, we take part in activities that involve the use of symbols that have special meaning to us. For example, at a birthday party, we put candles on a cake, sing the Birthday Song, ask the person who is turning a year older to make a wish and blow out the candles, and then cut the cake. We also bring wrapped gifts for the celebrant. Some of the activities which may be a part of a ritual include: eating, drinking, toasting, dancing, singing, exchanging gifts, bathing, wearing special clothing, playing games, reading aloud, offering blessings or good wishes, planting, burning, chanting, and praying.

We may include just one person, or hundreds, as we engage in a particular ritual. In the following case example, a woman chose to have several close friends present during the enactment of a ceremony she designed for forgiving her ex-husband and moving on with her life.

Marsha had been haunted by the bitter resentment she felt toward her ex-husband Larry, who had left her over ten years earlier for a younger woman. In therapy, Marsha came to realize that the hostile feelings she held for Larry were actually keeping her stuck, and poisoning her present life experience. She worked hard at letting go of the hurt and anger she had been harboring for so long. And her final step in forgiving Larry and releasing all of the pain she had been carrying regarding the divorce, was to design and carry out her own ritual. She wrote Larry a letter, explaining that she was choosing to let go of the bitterness she felt toward him so that she could move on with her life, thanking him for all of the valuable lessons he had taught her, for the good years they had together, and wishing him well in his life. Then she took her wedding ring, and asked a jeweler to re-set the diamond into a pendant she could wear as a necklace. She invited three close female friends to her house on the anniversary of her divorce. With all present gathered in a circle, Marsha read and then burned her letter to Larry. Next, Marsha expressed her appreciation to each friend for supporting her through this process. Then, Marsha brought out her new diamond pendant and passed it around. Each friend held it, offered her blessings, and spoke of her good wishes for Marsha from this day forward. Finally, Marsha put the pendant on a gold chain around her neck and affirmed her intention to enjoy her new life and welcome new experiences. They completed the celebration by sharing a meal and a bottle of fine wine, with a toast to Marsha's health and happiness.

A ritual of your own design can be a poignant way to underline your determination to forgive yourself and others and fully release the past. Your personal ceremony can serve as a transition point in your life, marking your passage from spellbound to free. Design your own ritual, using symbols and activities that are meaningful to you. You can invite as few or as many participants or witnesses as you wish. You can hold your rites in the privacy of your home, in a church or temple, on a mountaintop, in a forest clearing, or on the shore of an ocean or lake.

Remember, a ritual is a final step in the process of forgiveness. Imagine your surprise and delight, as you feel the deep and powerful internal shift that often results from participating in your own forgiveness ceremony.

CHAPTER SEVEN
RECEIVING LIFE'S BLESSINGS

As you awaken from your spellbound state, you gain easier access to the creative stream of universal energy that flows through your life like a great river. When you join that endless flow of well-being, you open to the unlimited blessings that life has to offer. You find yourself in the right place at the right time, living with greater ease, joy, and satisfaction. At times, it may even seem magical the way circumstances and events unfold with perfect timing, in alignment with your greatest hopes and fondest dreams. Your life becomes an enchanting journey, rather than a painful endurance test.

Living in the flow means retiring your life of struggle. You cease swimming against the current, and instead, allow it to transport you, easily and with far less effort, to your chosen destination. While you still act to accomplish your goals, those actions are fueled by inspiration, and fired by passion. You no longer waste energy trying to force yourself to do what you believe you should do. You discover a wellspring of motivation that propels you in whatever direction you want to go.

Letting go of struggle is not easy, when we have been accustomed to our ghosts urging us to struggle more, and convincing us that we have to prove our worthiness with blood, sweat, and tears. Yet, as the following example illustrates, it is only when we stop trying so hard to make things happen that things often significantly change for the better.

When I met Abby, she was in dire financial straits. On an impulse, she had quit her job two years earlier in order to build her own business. Since then, despite her best efforts to grow her business, her financial situation had progressively worsened. Although she did not spend money frivolously, she was barely holding on, and in imminent danger of losing her business and living out on the streets. She was deeply ashamed of having had credit cards revoked for lack of timely payment, bank accounts closed due to too many overdrawn checks, and collections agents calling to demand payment for her many debts. Abby had always been responsible with money, and wanted desperately to pay all of her bills. Yet nothing she had tried had improved her situation. In spite of all of her prayers and hard work, things were only getting worse.

Abby confessed that she worried constantly about her disastrous financial affairs; day and night, she agonized over her lack of money, and envisioned the most dire consequences. When she wasn't feeling guilty and ashamed about the past, she was living in fear of a catastrophic future.

I knew that for her financial situation to improve, Abby needed to let go of worry, guilt, and fear, and replace them with feelings of well-being. Rather than pushing so hard to try to make things better, she needed to allow good things into her life more easily. Abby had equated a lack of agony and struggle with being irresponsible about money.

With therapy and the use of many of the techniques described in this book, Abby eventually released her worries and fears and surrendered to the universal flow. As she placed her trust in a power greater than herself, she felt at peace for the first time in many months. Abby realized that letting go of the struggle meant being willing to follow the path that her inner guidance illuminated for her. As she recognized the urge to make a phone call or write a letter, she acted upon it. To Abby's surprise and delight, her financial situation began to improve within days of stopping her intensive effort to make it better. Paradoxically, it was only when she ceased trying so hard to create abundance that greater and greater amounts of money began to flow into her life in amazing ways. Within three months, Abby had all of the new business she could manage, her income had tripled, and she was well on her way to paying off all of her debts.

Let Go of Worries and Fear

Worry and fear are the result of trying to predict and control the future. They are your attempts at keeping yourself safe in an uncertain world. Although it may feel like you are helping yourself by being anxious about what lies ahead, the truth is that you are actually hurting yourself. Worry and fear are a good sign that you are trying to navigate the river of life by fighting the current. They are prime indicators that you are engaging in spellbound thinking, and thus, working against yourself in the accomplishment of your goals. Worry and fear tend to attract what you don't want, and repel what you do want. And while you are trying so hard to control the future, you are ignoring the one thing you have total control over, which is where you focus your attention in the present. This is your point of power.

If you catch yourself feeling worried or fearful about the future, ask yourself, "Is there something I can do about my concerns right now?" If there is, then go ahead and do it. If not, then let go of the worry and fear and imagine that things turn out just the way you want.

Befriend Your Desires

Often while we are haunted by our ghosts, we find that the best way to cope is by not having desires. Our inner tormentors convince us that we can't and/or don't deserve to have what we want, and so we try to feel better by dousing the flames of our passions. After all, if you pretend you don't want something, it doesn't hurt so much when you don't have it. We practice thinking small, and argue for our limitations. We adjust and accommodate to life's disappointments. And we stop believing that our situation will ever improve.

Yet, our deepest longings represent messages from our Spirit about our path of greatest joy and fulfillment in this lifetime. When we ignore our desires, we prevent ourselves from living the rich and satisfying lives we were meant to live. We stunt our personal growth. And we choose suffering with the status quo over risking an intoxicating ride on the powerful stream of well-being that flows through life.

Awakening from your spellbound state means becoming aware of your unlimited potential to do, be, and have whatever you desire in your life. It means beginning to direct the creative force within to consciously fashion the kind of life that thrills and delights you. You have the ability to stop surviving and to start thriving. It all begins when you allow your desires to light the way for you.

What Do You Desire?

Spend time asking yourself what it is you really want. How would you like yourself or your life to be different? You may wish for some form of material abundance, a life partner, perfect health, a different job, greater success in academics or sports, or perhaps something less tangible like greater freedom, more fun, more loving relationships, inner peace, creative inspiration, youthful vitality, or a deeper connection with your Spiritual source. Or, if you are not sure of what you want, you may desire greater clarity regarding what would make you happy, or clarity regarding the life path that would be in alignment with your higher purpose.

It is important not to censure yourself with thoughts that it isn't possible to meet your goal, that you have never been able to be/do/or have it before, or that you haven't the slightest idea about how to go about attaining what you desire. These are just echoes of the ghosts' messages. Instead, allow yourself to be honest about identifying what it is you really desire, no matter how impossible it may seem, or how hopeless you may feel about it.

Write down what it is you want, using positive, present tense sentences. For example, write, "I *have* a wonderful life partner who adores me," rather than, "I *will have* a wonderful life partner who adores me," or "I'm not alone anymore." You may wish to fill a large poster board with pictures you cut out of magazines, composing a collage, which represents your ideal future. Hang your collage in a private place, so it can remind you to focus daily on what you are creating for yourself.

Start to Dream about Getting What You Want

Once you have specified your desire, daydream about what it will be like when it becomes a part of your reality. Be playful and light-hearted as you invent future scenes in your head in which you have and enjoy whatever it is you want. Put yourself in those scenes, and imagine what it feels like to experience the fulfillment of your dreams. Get excited about what you envision. Make it as real as you can. Have fun conjuring up ever-more pleasing episodes in your future life story.

Sadly, many of us have been discouraged from visualizing our dreams by well-meaning parents and teachers who wanted to protect us from disappointment. They have cautioned us to "face reality" and "get our heads out of the clouds," as if our flights of fancy are a personality defect that must be eradicated. When in reality, everything we wish to attain in life begins in our imagination. We use our creative daydreaming to chart the course of our lives, prepare ourselves for the journey, recognize the signposts that point the way, and familiarize ourselves in advance with our destination. Imagining yourself being, doing, or having what you desire is the key that unlocks the door to manifesting your true desires.

Beware of the "Reality Rules" Thought Trap

Often the life we want is in direct contrast to the life we are living. We want perfect health, but we have a life-threatening disease. We want financial abundance, but we have an abundance of debt. We want freedom, but we feel imprisoned by our responsibilities. And herein lies your ghost's biggest weapon in keeping you stuck. Beware of the thought trap that says, "Reality Rules." This is the message from the phantoms that says you can't significantly change your current reality. If you are poor, you will always be poor. If you are alone, you will always be alone. If you are sick, you will always be sick.

Your ghosts may fortify their message by pointing to other times when you tried to change yourself or your life and seemingly failed. The relapses. The personal and professional rejections. The unhappy relationships. Anything to discourage you from believing in your power to create what you desire.

No matter what kind of life you are living today, it can be different tomorrow. Nothing in life is permanent. You have already made significant changes in your life that have been positive and life-affirming. You may wish to take a moment and write down all of the changes, big and small, you have made for the better throughout your life. And then, remind yourself that you can do it again.

The key is to deal with the present-moment reality of your life, without becoming seduced into thinking this is all there is. Remember that your life is a journey, and this is just one brief, stopping point along the way. For any aspect of your life that does not please you, focus on where you want to go next, instead of where you are or have been. Realize that there are unlimited possibilities stretching before you in every direction. If you end up choosing a route that doesn't bring you joy, you can always change your course.

Focus on the Essence of What You Want

As you imagine what it is you want, it is best to focus on the *essence* of what you desire, rather than the *form*. For example, if you desire a new job, focus on the qualities you would like in your work environment, the kind of work you would like to be doing, the kinds of relationships you would like to have with your co-workers, and how you want to feel at work. This is the essence of the new job. In contrast, avoid focusing on the form—which would be working for a particular company in a particular building. When you want to create something very specific in your life—such as an intimate relationship with a particular person—it may trigger more fear and doubt than confidence, as you imagine it. Because of this, it is better to imagine yourself in an intimate relationship that is ideal for you in every way, and to be open to the right person showing up at the right time in your life. If the person you are interested in is the right one for you, know that the relationship will unfold perfectly. Rather than limiting yourself, let your Inner Being help you to find the right match for the essence of what you want. It will be even better than any specific thing you have in mind.

Think about Why You Want It

Spend time thinking about how whatever you want will enrich your life and the lives of others, and enable you to develop higher qualities, such as love, wisdom, courage, joy, self-appreciation, generosity, and compassion. How will having what you desire make you a better person? In what ways will it enable you to grow and develop yourself? What do you hope to learn from the experience? How will it foster your spiritual development? Are there any ways in which you will be able to make the world a better place by creating what you desire? Focus on the ways in which the manifestation of your desires will be a source of personal growth and enable you to bring more light to the world.

Demonstrate the qualities today that you are hoping to attain with the fulfillment of your desires. For example, if you think having a special relationship will make you a more loving person, find new ways to express more love today. If you believe that having a better job will make you feel happier and more secure, try to feel happier and more secure now. Perhaps you believe that having more money in the bank will enable you to feel more free and be more generous. Dare to feel more free and demonstrate greater generosity in this moment. If you think losing weight will help you to accept yourself, begin to think and act in a more self-accepting manner while still at your present weight. Be the kind of person you hope to become when your dreams come true, and watch your life change for the better.

Harmonize Your Energy with Your Desires

Play with the image of achieving your goal until it feels perfectly natural and normal to have what you desire. Envision what it will be like to have what you want, until you and your desires are in perfect harmony. How do you know when you have accomplished this? When imagining yourself being, doing, or having what you want generates no uncomfortable feelings or reactions. No doubts, no anxiety, no fears, no frustration. You know you deserve to have it, and you can easily picture yourself having or attaining it. And, only positive feelings are associated with having your dreams come true.

A good way to identify what it feels like to be in harmony with what you want is to think of something positive that you easily allow into your life. It can be as simple as delicious food on your dinner plate, or a hug from your best friend. When you think of this thing you easily accept, notice how you feel inside. Experience it fully, in all its emotional richness. Then try to capture that same feeling when you think about whatever you want to create in your life.

The following exercise is a fun way to practice being in harmony with the manifestation of your desires. You will need a partner to do this exercise.

Exercise #20
The Future Encounter

1. Pretend that you and your exercise partner haven't seen each other for one year or more (specify the number of years before you begin), and since you last met, each of you has accomplished all of your goals. Every one of your dreams is now a reality.

2. Taking turns, tell each other about all of the wonderful changes in your lives, while the listener expresses excitement and asks questions: "What does it feel like to have the relationship you always wanted?" Or, "How does it feel to be in perfect health?"

3. Have fun speaking as if you already have and enjoy everything you have been wanting. Be bold, playful, and outrageous as you describe the ideal life you are now living.

I once had a group of people who suffer from severe chronic pain do this exercise for ten minutes. Many of the group members were surprised to note that they did not feel any pain by the end of the exercise. You too, will find yourself flooded with positive energy as you engage your desires in this way.

Tune into and Follow Your Inner Guidance

Once you have begun to imagine what you want to manifest in your life, begin to follow those urges to take action which bubble up within you. It is as if you are on a treasure hunt, and the clues for which direction to go are offered to you, one-by-one, on the inner plane. At times it may not be clear how following these inner urgings will lead you to your intended goal. Making a phone call, sending an e-mail, visiting a friend or relative, attending a class or workshop, joining a club, traveling to a new place, speaking to an interesting stranger, or reading a particular book may, to your surprise, take you one step closer to living out your dreams.

Your inner guidance will always lead you toward your intended destination, rather than away from something that is not right for you. The messages from your Spiritual Essence will be gentle nudges, rather than aggressive shoves in a particular direction. Whenever you feel yourself particularly motivated or inspired to do something, your Inner Being is letting you know that you are on track. Do what makes you happy, and it will lead to the fulfillment of your fondest desires.

Trust That All Is Well

Having faith means choosing to trust that all will work out in accordance with your highest good. It means believing that if you surrender to the river of life, it will carry you safely to your chosen destination. Perhaps you have already had the experience of trusting your Spiritual Essence to guide you towards your best possible future. Somehow you just knew which way to go at life's intersecting points, so you ended up exactly where you had hoped to be, or someplace even better. When we go with the flow, we move in harmony with the music of our Spirit. Rather than struggling to reach our destination, our focus is on enjoying the journey. Rather than being fearful of what might lie around the next bend, we feel light-hearted and open to life's surprises. We anticipate good things for ourselves, holding the expectation that our lives are unfolding in perfect alignment with our desires.

The following guided visualization will assist you in surrendering to your highest good as you let go of struggle.

Exercise #21
Opening to Receive Life's Blessings

1. Put your body in a comfortable position, close your eyes, and begin to breathe deeply. Find yourself again in the soothing, nurturing safety and comfort of your heart sanctuary. Picture its smells, sights, sounds, and sensations. Feel divine peace emanating throughout this sacred space.

2. Imagine that there is a magnificent river of light flowing into your heart sanctuary that carries everything you are wanting directly to you. There is nothing for you to do, but allow your highest good to come to you, easily and effortlessly, via this endless stream of positive energy. You needn't even know what your highest good looks like. Just invite it into your heart sanctuary, and know that it will be perfect for you in every way.

3. Picture all that you desire filling your heart sanctuary, as you open to receive abundance of every kind. Imagine that everything you have attracted brings more light into your life. Feel yourself becoming even more radiant as you harmonize your light with the many blessings that surround you.

4. Feel free to remain in your heart sanctuary for as long as you like. When you are ready, return to your present time and space feeling clear-headed, refreshed, and alert.

Enjoy What You Already Have

The most important element in receiving life's blessings is to appreciate and enjoy what you already have. Once you have identified what you want to create in your life, and have imagined yourself having it, refocus your attention on the things that make you happy in your life today. Let your life be a joyous adventure, in which each day brings new delights. Get happy. Lighten up. Have fun every day. Do things to make each day special for yourself and others. Pay attention to the many good things in your life today. Take time each day to count your blessings, and they will continue to multiply.

AFTERWORD

As you use this handbook to awaken from your spell, remember that our lives follow seasons like the Earth that sustains us. When you are in a winter mode, you may feel frozen and barren, and wonder if there will ever be a time of new growth. Or you may feel peaceful and content, hibernating for a while in preparation for the coming spring. Even though it appears as if there is nothing much going on during your wintertime, seeds of change are taking root beneath the surface. A winter may last weeks, months, or years for you. But eventually, spring always arrives, bringing glorious color and an explosion of new creativity and life. Spring is when you begin to enjoy the results of cultivating new ways of thinking, feeling, and behaving. By summertime, you are basking in the light of your spiritual unfolding, like a beautiful flower whose petals are drinking in the sun's life-giving rays. With the coming of fall, enjoy the harvest that already bears the seeds for the new planting. While the old is slowly dying off, new opportunities appear for planting these seeds in the fertile soil of your consciousness. And then, of course, another winter arrives.

Find pleasure in each season in your journey toward greater aliveness and wholeness. Be gentle with yourself. Learn to move according to your own rhythm, doing what feels right and good to you at your own pace. Take your time and savor the delight and perfection of wherever you are in nature's gentle unfolding.

The processes in this book are designed to be used again and again, as you experience the ebb and flow of consciousness that accompanies your life's seasonal changes. Let this book accompany you in the darkest winter and the brightest summer. Let it guide you back to your Deeper Self, should you temporarily find yourself lost in a storm of emotion. Use it to rake away the dead leaves of fall, and to recognize the first tiny buds on a young tree in the early spring. Let it remind you to celebrate yourself, and your profound connection to all of Life. May it help you to awaken to who you really are—Love itself.

REFERENCES

Cameron, Julia and Mark Bryan. *The Artist's Way: A Spiritual Path to Higher Creativity*. New York: Tarcher/Putnam, 1992.

Dossey, Larry. *Healing Words: The Power of Prayer and the Practice of Medicine*. San Francisco: Harper Collins, 1993.

Goulding, Mary and Robert Goulding. *Changing Lives Through Redecision Therapy*. New York: Grove Press, 1997.

Hicks, Esther and Jerry Hicks. *A New Beginning I: Handbook for Joyous Survival*. San Antonio, TX: Abraham-Hicks Publications, 1988.

Hicks, Esther and Jerry Hicks. *A New Beginning II: A Personal Handbook to Enhance Your Life, Liberty, and Pursuit of Happiness*. San Antonio, TX: Abraham-Hicks Publications, 1991.

Huffines, La Una. *Bridge of Light: Tools of Light For Spiritual Transformation*. New York: Simon and Schuster, 1989.

Myss, Carolyn. *Why People Don't Heal and How They Can*. New York: Three Rivers Press, 1997.

Roman, Sanaya. *Living with Joy: Keys to Personal Power and Spiritual Transformation*. Tiburon, CA: H.J. Kramer, 1986.

Roman, Sanaya. *Spiritual Growth: Being Your Higher Self*. Tiburon, CA: H.J. Kramer, 1989.

Tolle, Eckhart. *The Power of Now*. Novato, CA: New World Library, 1999.

Recommended Music for Guided Visualizations

Hilary Stagg:
Dream Spiral
Sweet Return
Feather Light

Mike Rowland:
The Fairy Ring
Silver Wings
My Elfin Friends
And So to Dream

2002:
Chrysalis
Land of Forever
River of Stars
Across an Ocean of Dreams

Ray Lynch:
Sky of Mind

Lazaris Music:
Journey with Lazaris
Lazaris Remembers Lemuria

For information about workshops offered by Dr. Eve Delunas and Lightwork Visions Enterprises, visit our web site at:

www.lightworkvisions.com

To arrange for Dr. Delunas to speak to your group, please contact us at:

Lightwork Visions Enterprises
P.O. Box 221520
Carmel, CA 93922
(831) 484-5983

LIGHTWORK VISIONS
ENTERPRISES

ALSO AVAILABLE FROM LIGHTWORK VISIONS:

*Guided Visualizations for Breaking the Spell of the Past
and Entering the Joyous Now* by Eve Delunas, Ph.D.
A set of compact discs created as a companion to *Breaking the
Spell of the Past: Entering the Joyous Now*, on which the author
guides you through the visualization exercises presented in the
book. $40.00

Lightwork: A Course For Spiritual Enlightenment by Joyia Felice
This book provides you with tools for stepping into a greater role
of world service and fulfilling your higher purpose by becoming
an enlightened Lightworker. ISBN 0-9742284-0-0 $20.00

Journey Toward Lightwork by Joyia Felice
A collection of spiritual readings that have been received over a
period of 30 years in the life of a mystic. These lessons provide
the foundation for her book, *Lightwork: A Course For Spiritual
Enlightenment*. ISBN 0-9742284-2-7 $18.00

Lightworker Prayers and Meditations
by Joyia Felice and Eve Delunas, Ph.D.
A compilation of readings, meditations, and prayers
for the upliftment of self, humanity, and all life.
ISBN 0-9742284-3-5 $15.00

ORDER FORM

Fax Orders: (831) 484-5983 Send this form.

Telephone Orders: (831) 484-LWVE or (831) 484-5983
Have your credit card ready.

Email Orders: www.lightworkvisions.com

Postal Orders: Lightwork Visions Enterprises
P.O. Box 221520 Carmel, CA 93922

Name:_____

Address: _____

City: _____ State: _____ Zip:_____

Telephone: _____ Fax: _____

Email address: _____

Qty	Item	Price Each	Total
____	_____	_____	_____
____	_____	_____	_____
____	_____	_____	_____

Sales Tax: Please add 7.25% for CA residents.

Air Shipping:
U.S.: $5.00 for first item;
    $2.00 for each additional item.
International: Please call for rates.

Subtotal _____

CA Sales Tax _____

Shipping & Handling _____

Total _____

Payment:

❏ check   credit card: ❏ Visa ❏ MasterCard ❏ AMEX ❏ Discover

Card number _____ Exp. Date: _____

Name on Card _____

Cardholder Signature _____

Please send more information on:

❏ Other books and CDs ❏ Speaking/Seminars ❏ Lightwork Visions Workshops